King Henry the 6th Part 3

By William Shakespeare

Edited by Julien Coallier

Copyright Julien Coallier 2012

All Rights Reserved.

Characters

All

Bona, sister to the French Queen

Duke of Exeter, uncle to Henry IV, great-uncle to Henry V

Duke of Norfolk

Duke/Earl of Somerset, John Beaufort

Earl of Northumberland

Earl of Pembroke

Earl of Warwick

Earl of Westmoreland

Earl of Westmoreland

Earl Oxford

Edmond, Earl of Rutland

Edmund Mortimer, Earl of March

Father, who has killed his son

First Keeper

First Messenger

First Watchman

George Plantagenet (Duke of Clarence)

Henry VI

Henry, Earl of Richmond, a youth

Huntsman

King Edward IV (Plantagenet)

King Lewis XI, king of France

Lieutenant, of the Tower

Lord (Earl) Rivers, brother to Lady Gray (Queen Elizabeth)

Lord Clifford

Lord Hastings

Lord Stafford

Marquess of Montague

Mayor of York

Messenger

Nobleman

Post

Prince Edward

Queen Elizabeth, starts as Lady Grey, marries Edward IV

Queen Margaret, daughter to Reignier, afterwards married to King Henry VI

Richard III (Duke of Gloucester), son of Richard Plantagenet, duke of York; was duke of Gloucester before enthronement

Richard Plantagenet (Duke of Gloucester), becomes duke of York in Henry VI, Part

Second Keeper

Second Messenger

Second Watchman

Sir Hugh Mortimer, uncle to the Duke of York

Sir John Montgomery

Sir John Mortimer, uncle to the Duke of York

Sir John Somerville

Sir William Stanley, called also Earl of Derby

Soldier

Son, who has killed his father

Third Watchman

Tutor of Rutland

Scenes

Act I – Page 9

Scene 1. London. The Parliament-house.

Scene 2. Sandal Castle.

Scene 3. Field of battle betwixt Sandal Castle and Wakefield.

Scene 4. Another part of the field.

Act II – Page 51

Scene 1. A plain near Mortimer's Cross in Herefordshire.

Scene 2. Before York.

Scene 3. A field of battle between Towton and Saxton, in

Scene 4. Another part of the field.

Scene 5. Another part of the field.

Scene 6. Another part of the field.

Act III – Page 93

Scene 1. A forest in the north of England.

Scene 2. London. The palace.

Scene 3. France. King Lewis XI's palace.

Act IV – Page 131

Scene 1. London. The palace.

Scene 2. A plain in Warwickshire.

Scene 3. Edward's camp, near Warwick.

Scene 4. London. The palace.

Scene 5. A park near Middleham Castle In Yorkshire.

Scene 6. London. The Tower.

Scene 7. Before York.

Scene 8. London. The palace.

Act V – Page 173

Scene 1. Coventry.

Scene 2. A field of battle near Barnet.

Scene 3. Another part of the field.

Scene 4. Plains near Tewksbury.

Scene 5. Another part of the field.

Scene 6. London. The Tower.

Scene 7. London. The palace.

Act 1 Scene 1

London. The Parliament-house.

(Alarum)

(York, Edward, Richard, Norfolk, Montague, Warwick, and Soldiers enter)

Warwick

I wonder how the king escaped our hands.

York

While we pursued the horsemen of the north, he slyly stole away and left his men at the great Lord of Northumberland, whose warlike ears could never brook retreat, cheered up the drooping army

Himself Lord Clifford and Lord Stafford, all abreast, charged our main battle's front, and breaking in were by the swords of common soldiers slain.

Edward

Lord Stafford's father, Duke of Buckingham, is either slain or wounded dangerously

I cleft his beaver with a downright blow, that this is true father, behold his blood.

Montague

And brother, here's the Earl of Wiltshire's blood, whom I encountered as the battles joined.

Richard

Speak thou for me and tell them what I did.

(Throwing down Somerset's head)

York

Richard hath best deserved of all my sons.

But is your grace dead, my Lord of Somerset?

Norfolk

Such hope have all the line of John of Gaunt!

Richard

Thus do I hope to shake King Henry's head.

Warwick

And so do I. Victorious Prince of York, before I see thee seated in that throne, which now the house of Lancaster has taken, I vow by heaven these eyes shall never close.

This is the palace of the fearful king and this the regal seat, possess it York

For this is thine and not King Henry's heirs'

York

Assist me, then, sweet Warwick and I will

For hither we have broken in by force.

Norfolk

We'll all assist you

He that flies shall die.

York

Thanks, gentle Norfolk, stay by me my lords

Soldiers stay and lodge by me this night.

They go up

Warwick

And when the king comes, offer no violence, unless he seek to thrust you out perforce.

York

The queen this day here holds her parliament, but little thinks we shall be of her council, by words or blows here let us win our right.

Richard

Armed as we are, let's stay within this house.

Warwick

The bloody parliament shall this be called, unless Plantagenet, Duke of York, be king and bashful Henry deposed, whose cowardice hath made us by-words to our enemies.

York

Then leave me not, my lords; be resolute

I mean to take possession of my right.

Warwick

Neither the king, nor he that loves him best, the proudest he that holds up Lancaster, dares stir a wing if Warwick shake his bells.

I'll plant Plantagenet, root him up who dares, resolve thee, Richard Claim the English crown.

(Flourish)

(King Henry VI, Clifford, Northumberland, Westmoreland, Exeter, and the rest enter)

King Henry VI

My lords, look where the sturdy rebel sits, even in the chair of state, belike he means backed by the power of Warwick that false peer, to aspire unto the crown and reign as king.

Earl of Northumberland, he slew thy father.

And thine, Lord Clifford

You both have vowed revenge on him, his sons, his favourites and his friends.

Northumberland

If I be not, heavens be revenged on me!

Clifford

The hope thereof makes Clifford mourn in steel.

Westmoreland

What, shall we suffer this? let's pluck him down, my heart for anger burns; I cannot brook it.

King Henry VI

Be patient, gentle Earl of Westmoreland.

Clifford

Patience is for poltroons, such as he, he durst not sit there, had your father lived.

My gracious lord, here in the parliament let us assail the family of York.

Northumberland

Well hast thou spoken, cousin: be it so.

King Henry VI

Ah, know you not the city favours them and they have troops of soldiers at their beck?

Exeter

But when the duke is slain, they'll quickly fly.

King Henry VI

Far be the thought of this from Henry's heart to make a shambles of the parliament-house!

Cousin of Exeter, frowns, words and threats shall be the war that Henry means to use.

Thou factious Duke of York, descend my throne and kneel for grace and mercy at my feet

I am thy sovereign.

York

I am thine.

Exeter

For shame, come down: he made thee Duke of York.

York

It was my inheritance, as the earldom was.

Exeter

Thy father was a traitor to the crown.

Warwick

Exeter, thou art a traitor to the crown in following this usurping Henry.

Clifford

Whom should he follow but his natural king?

Warwick

True, Clifford

That's Richard Duke of York.

King Henry VI

And shall I stand, and thou sit in my throne?

York

It must and shall be so, content thyself.

Warwick

Be Duke of Lancaster; let him be king.

Westmoreland

He is both king and Duke of Lancaster

That the Lord of Westmoreland shall maintain.

Warwick

And Warwick shall disprove it.

You forget that we are those which chased you from the field and slew your fathers, and with colours spread marched through the city to the palace gates.

Northumberland

Yes, Warwick, I remember it to my grief

By his soul, thou and thy house shall rue it.

Westmoreland

Plantagenet, of thee and these thy sons, thy kinsman and thy friends, I'll have more lives than drops of blood were in my father's veins.

Clifford

Urge it no more; lest that, instead of words, I send thee, Warwick, such a messenger as shall revenge his death before I stir.

Warwick

Poor Clifford! how I scorn his worthless threats!

York

Will you we show our title to the crown?

If not, our swords shall plead it in the field.

King Henry VI

What title hast thou, traitor, to the crown?

Thy father was, as thou art, Duke of York

Thy grandfather, Roger Mortimer, Earl of March, I am the son of Henry the Fifth, who made the Dauphin and the French to stoop and seized upon their towns and provinces.

Warwick

Talk not of France, sith thou hast lost it all.

King Henry VI

The lord protector lost it, and not I, when I was crowned I was but nine months old.

Richard

You are old enough now, and yet, methinks, you lose.

Father, tear the crown from the usurper's head.

Edward

Sweet father, do so

Set it on your head.

Montague

Good brother, as thou lovest and honourest arms, let's fight it out and not stand cavilling thus.

Richard

Sound drums and trumpets, and the king will fly.

York

Sons, peace!

King Henry VI

Peace, thou! and give King Henry leave to speak.

Warwick

Plantagenet shall speak first: hear him, lords

Be you silent and attentive too, for he that interrupts him shall not live.

King Henry VI

Think'st thou that I will leave my kingly throne, wherein my grandsire and my father sat?

No, first shall war unpeople this my realm

Ay, and their colours, often borne in France and now in England to our heart's great sorrow shall be my winding-sheet.

Why faint you, lords?

My title's good, and better far than his.

Warwick

Prove it, Henry, and thou shalt be king.

King Henry VI

Henry the Fourth by conquest got the crown.

York

It 'was by rebellion against his king.

King Henry VI

(From Aside) I know not what to say; my title's weak...

Tell me, may not a king adopt an heir?

York

What then?

King Henry VI

An if he may, than am I lawful king

For Richard, in the view of many lords resigned the crown to Henry the Fourth, whose heir my father was, and I am his.

York

He rose against him, being his sovereign and made him to resign his crown perforce.

Warwick

Suppose, my lords, he did it unconstrained, think you it were prejudicial to his crown?

Exeter

No

He could not so resign his crown but that the next heir should succeed and reign.

King Henry VI

Art thou against us, Duke of Exeter?

Exeter

His is the right, and therefore pardon me.

York

Why whisper you, my lords, and answer not?

Exeter

My conscience tells me he is lawful king.

King Henry VI

(From Aside) All will revolt from me, and turn to him.

Northumberland

Plantagenet, for all the claim thou lay'st, think not that Henry shall be so deposed.

Warwick

Deposed he shall be, in despite of all.

Northumberland

Thou art deceived, it is not thy southern power of Essex, Norfolk, Suffolk, nor of Kent, can set the duke up in despite of me, which makes thee thus presumptuous and proud

Clifford

King Henry, be thy title right or wrong, Lord Clifford vows to fight in thy defence, may that ground gape and swallow me alive, where I shall kneel to him that slew my father!

King Henry VI

Oh Clifford, how thy words revive my heart!

York

Henry of Lancaster, resign thy crown.

What mutter you, or what conspire you, lords?

Warwick

Do right unto this princely Duke of York, or I will fill the house with armed men and over the chair of state where now he sits, write up his title with usurping blood.

He stamps with his foot and the soldiers show themselves

King Henry VI

My Lord of Warwick, hear me but one word, let me for this my lifetime reign as king.

York

Confirm the crown to me and to mine heirs, and thou shalt reign in quiet while thou livest.

King Henry VI

I am content, Richard Plantagenet, enjoy the kingdom after my decease.

Clifford

What wrong is this unto the prince your son!

Warwick

What good is this to England and himself!

Westmoreland

Base, fearful and despairing Henry!

Clifford

How hast thou injured both thyself and us!

Westmoreland

I cannot stay to hear these articles.

Northumberland

Nor I.

Clifford

Come, cousin, let us tell the queen these news.

Westmoreland

Farewell, faint-hearted and degenerate king, in whose cold blood no spark of honour bides.

Northumberland

Be thou a prey unto the house of York and die in bands for this unmanly deed!

Clifford

In dreadful war mayst thou be overcome, or live in peace abandon'd and despised!

(Northumberland, Clifford, and Westmoreland exit)

Warwick

Turn this way, Henry, and regard them not.

Exeter

They seek revenge and therefore will not yield.

King Henry VI

Ah, Exeter!

Warwick

Why should you sigh, my lord?

King Henry VI

Not for myself, Lord Warwick, but my son whom I unnaturally shall disinherit.

But be it as it may, I here entail the crown to thee and to thine heirs for ever

Conditionally, that here thou take an oath to cease this civil war, and whilst I live to honour me as thy king and sovereign, and neither by treason nor hostility to seek to put me down and reign thyself

York

This oath I willingly take and will perform.

Warwick

Long live King Henry! Plantagenet embrace him.

King Henry VI

And long live thou and these thy forward sons!

York

Now York and Lancaster are reconciled.

Exeter

Accursed be he that seeks to make them foes!

(Sennet)

Here they come down

York

Farewell, my gracious lord; I'll to my castle.

Warwick

And I'll keep London with my soldiers.

Norfolk

And I to Norfolk with my followers.

Montague

And I unto the sea from whence I came.

(York, Edward, Edmund, George, Richard, Warwick, Norfolk, Montague, their Soldiers, and Attendants exit)

King Henry VI

And I, with grief and sorrow, to the court.

(Queen Margaret and Prince Edward enter)

Exeter

Here comes the queen, whose looks bewray her anger:

I'll steal away.

King Henry VI

Exeter, so will I.

Queen Margaret

Nay, go not from me; I will follow thee.

King Henry VI

Be patient, gentle queen, and I will stay.

Queen Margaret

Who can be patient in such extremes?

Ah, wretched man! would I had died a maid and never seen thee, never borne thee son, seeing thou hast proved so unnatural a father hath he deserved to lose his birthright thus?

Hadst thou but loved him half so well as I, or felt that pain which I did for him once, or nourished him as I did with my blood thou wouldst have left thy dearest heart-blood there

Rather than have that savage duke thine heir and disinherited thine only son.

Prince Edward

Father, you cannot disinherit me, if you be king, why should not I succeed?

King Henry VI

Pardon me, Margaret

Pardon me, sweet son, the Earl of Warwick and the duke enforced me.

Queen Margaret

Enforced thee! art thou king, and wilt be forced?

I shame to hear thee speak. Ah, timorous wretch!

Thou hast undone thyself, thy son and me

Given unto the house of York such head as thou shalt reign but by their sufferance.

To entail him and his heirs unto the crown, what is it but to make thy sepulchre and creep into it far before thy time?

Warwick is chancellor and the lord of Calais

Stern Falconbridge commands the narrow seas

The duke is made protector of the realm

And yet shalt thou be safe? such safety finds the trembling lamb environed with wolves.

Had I been there, which am a silly woman, the soldiers should have tossed me on their pikes before I would have granted to that act.

But thou preferr'st thy life before thine honour, and seeing thou dost, I here divorce myself both from thy table, Henry, and thy bed, until that act of parliament be repealed, whereby my son is disinherited.

The northern lords, that have forsworn thy colours, will follow mine, if once they see them spread

Spread they shall be, to thy foul disgrace and utter ruin of the house of York.

Thus do I leave thee.

Come, son, let's away

Our army is ready

Come, we'll after them.

King Henry VI

Stay, gentle Margaret, and hear me speak.

Queen Margaret

Thou hast spoke too much already

Get thee gone.

King Henry VI

Gentle son Edward, thou wilt stay with me?

Queen Margaret

Ay, to be murdered by his enemies.

Prince Edward

When I return with victory from the field I'll see your grace, till then I'll follow her.

Queen Margaret

Come, son, away

We may not linger thus.

(Queen Margaret and Prince Edward exit)

King Henry VI

Poor queen! How love to me and to her son hath made her break out into terms of rage!

Revenged may she be on that hateful duke, whose haughty spirit winged with desire, will cost my crown and like an empty eagle tire on the flesh of me and of my son!

The loss of those three lords torments my heart, I'll write unto them and entreat them fair.

Come, cousin you shall be the messenger.

Exeter

And I, I hope, shall reconcile them all.

(Exit)

Act 1 Scene 2

Sandal Castle.

(Richard, Edward, and Montague enter)

Richard

Brother, though I be youngest, give me leave.

Edward

No, I can better play the orator.

Montague

But I have reasons strong and forcible.

(York enters)

York

Why, how now, sons and brother! at a strife?

What is your quarrel? how began it first?

Edward

No quarrel, but a slight contention.

York

About what?

Richard

About that which concerns your grace and us

The crown of England, father, which is yours.

York

Mine boy? not till King Henry be dead.

Richard

Your right depends not on his life or death.

Edward

Now you are heir, therefore enjoy it now by giving the house of Lancaster leave to breathe, it will outrun you father, in the end.

York

I took an oath that he should quietly reign.

Edward

But for a kingdom any oath may be broken, I would break a thousand oaths to reign one year.

Richard

No

God forbid your grace should be forsworn.

York

I shall be, if I claim by open war.

Richard

I'll prove the contrary, if you'll hear me speak.

York

Thou canst not, son; it is impossible.

Richard

And oath is of no moment, being not took before a true and lawful magistrate that hath authority over him that swears, Henry had none but did take the place

Then, seeing it was he that made you to depose your oath, my lord is vain and frivolous.

Therefore to arms! And father, do but think how sweet a thing it is to wear a crown

Within whose circuit is Elysium and all that poets feign of bliss and joy.

Why do we finger thus? I cannot rest until the white rose that I wear be dyed, even in the lukewarm blood of Henry's heart.

York

Richard, enough

I will be king, or die.

Brother, thou shalt to London presently and whet on Warwick to this enterprise.

Thou Richard, shalt to the Duke of Norfolk and tell him privately of our intent.

You Edward, shall unto my Lord Cobham, with whom the Kentishmen will willingly rise, in them I trust

They are soldiers, witty, courteous, liberal, full of spirit.

While you are thus employed, what resteth more but that I seek occasion how to rise, and yet the king not privy to my drift nor any of the house of Lancaster?

(A Messenger enters)

But stay, what news?

Why comest thou in such post?

Messenger

The queen with all the northern earls and lords intend here to besiege you in your castle, she is hard by with twenty thousand men

Therefore fortify your hold, my lord.

York

Ay, with my sword. What! think'st thou that we fear them?

Edward and Richard, you shall stay with me

My brother Montague shall post to London, let noble Warwick, Cobham, and the rest, whom we have left protectors of the king with powerful policy, strengthen themselves

And trust not simple Henry nor his oaths.

Montague

Brother, I go

I'll win them, fear it not, and thus most humbly I do take my leave.

(Exit)

(John Mortimer and Hugh Mortimer enter)

Sir John and Sir Hugh Mortimer, mine uncles, you are come to Sandal in a happy hour

The army of the queen mean to besiege us.

John Mortimer

She shall not need

We'll meet her in the field.

York

What, with five thousand men?

Richard

Ay, with five hundred, father, for a need, a woman's general, what should we fear?

(A march afar off)

Edward

I hear their drums, let's set our men in order and issue forth and bid them battle straight.

York

Five men to twenty!

Though the odds be great, I doubt not, uncle, of our victory.

Many a battle have I won in France, when as the enemy hath been ten to one, why should I not now have the like success?

(Alarum)

(Exit)

Act 1 Scene 3

Field of battle between Sandal Castle and Wakefield.

(Alarums)

(Rutland and his Tutor enter)

Rutland

Ah, whither shall I fly to escape their hands?

Ah, tutor, look where bloody Clifford comes!

(Clifford and Soldiers enter)

Clifford

Chaplain, away! thy priesthood saves thy life.

As for the brat of this accursed duke, whose father slew my father, he shall die.

Tutor

And I, my lord, will bear him company.

Clifford

Soldiers, away with him!

Tutor

Ah, Clifford, murder not this innocent child, lest thou be hated both of God and man!

(Exits dragged off by Soldiers)

Clifford

How now! is he dead already? or is it fear that makes him close his eyes?

I'll open them.

Rutland

So looks the pent-up lion o'er the wretch that trembles under his devouring paws

So he walks, insulting over his prey, and so he comes to rend his limbs asunder.

Ah, gentle Clifford, kill me with thy sword and not with such a cruel threatening look.

Sweet Clifford, hear me speak before I die.

I am too mean a subject for thy wrath, be thou revenged on men, and let me live.

Clifford

In vain thou speak'st, poor boy

My father's blood hath stopped the passage where thy words should enter.

Rutland

Then let my father's blood open it again, he is a man and Clifford cope with him.

Clifford

Had thy brethren here, their lives and thine were not revenge sufficient for me

No, if I digged up thy forefathers' graves and hung their rotten coffins up in chains, it could not slake mine ire, nor ease my heart.

The sight of any of the house of York is as a fury to torment my soul

Till I root out their accursed line and leave not one alive, I live in hell.

Therefore…

(Lifting his hand)

Rutland

Oh let me pray before I take my death!

To thee I pray

Sweet Clifford, pity me!

Clifford

Such pity as my rapier's point affords.

Rutland

I never did thee harm: why wilt thou slay me?

Clifford

Thy father hath.

Rutland

But it was were I was born.

Thou hast one son

His sake pity me, lest in revenge thereof sith God is just, he be as miserably slain as I.

Ah, let me live in prison all my days

When I give occasion of offence, then let me die, for now thou hast no cause.

Clifford

No cause!

Thy father slew my father; therefore, die.

(Stabs him)

Rutland

May the gods cause this action to be that which makes you best known

(Dies)

Clifford

Plantagenet! I come, Plantagenet!

And this thy son's blood cleaving to my blade shall rust upon my weapon, till thy blood, congealed with this, do make me wipe off both. **(Exit)**

Act 1 Scene 4

Another part of the field.

(Alarum)

(York enters)

York

The army of the queen hath got the field, my uncles both are slain in rescuing me

All my followers to the eager foe turn back and fly, like ships before the wind or lambs pursued by hunger-starved wolves.

My sons, God knows what hath bechanced them, but this I know, they have demeaned themselves like men born to renown by life or death.

Three times did Richard make a lane to me.

And thrice cried courage father! fight it out! and full as oft came Edward to my side with purple falchion, painted to the hilt in blood of those that had encountered him, and when the hardiest warriors did retire, Richard cried Charge! and give no foot of ground!'

And cried a crown, or else a glorious tomb!

A sceptre, or an earthly sepulchre!'

With this, we charged again, but out, alas!

We bodged again

I have seen a swan with bootless labour swim against the tide and spend her strength with over-matching waves.

(A short alarum within)

Ah, hark! the fatal followers do pursue

I am faint and cannot fly their fury, and were I strong I would not shun their fury, the sands are numbered that make up my life

Here must I stay, and here my life must end.

(Queen Margaret, Clifford, Northumberland, Prince Edward, and Soldiers enter)

Come, bloody Clifford, rough Northumberland, I dare your quenchless fury to more rage, I am your butt and I abide your shot.

Northumberland

Yield to our mercy, proud Plantagenet.

Clifford

Ay, to such mercy as his ruthless arm, with downright payment showed unto my father.

Now Phaethon hath tumbled from his car and made an evening at the noontide prick.

York

My ashes, as the phoenix, may bring forth a bird that will revenge upon you all and in that hope I throw mine eyes to heaven scorning whate'er you can afflict me with.

Why come you not? what! multitudes, and fear?

Clifford

So cowards fight when they can fly no further

So doves do peck the falcon's piercing talons

So desperate thieves, all hopeless of their lives, breathe out invectives against the officers

York

Oh Clifford, but bethink thee once again, and in thy thought over-run my former time

And, if though canst for blushing, view this face, and bite thy tongue that slanders him with cowardice whose frown hath made thee faint and fly ere this!

Clifford

I will not bandy with thee word for word, but buckle with thee blows, twice two for one.

Queen Margaret

Hold, valiant Clifford! for a thousand causes I would prolong awhile the traitor's life.

Wrath makes him deaf, speak thou, Northumberland.

Northumberland

Hold, Clifford! do not honour him so much to prick thy finger, though to wound his heart, what valour were it, when a cur doth grin,

For one to thrust his hand between his teeth when he might spurn him with his foot away?

It is war's prize to take all vantages

Ten to one is no impeach of valour.

They lay hands on York, who struggles

Clifford

Ay, ay, so strives the woodcock with the gin.

Northumberland

So doth the cony struggle in the net.

York

So triumph thieves upon their conquered booty

True men yield, with robbers so overmatched.

Northumberland

What would your grace have done unto him now?

Queen Margaret

Brave warriors, Clifford and Northumberland, come, make him stand upon this molehill here, though naught at mountains with outstretched arms, yet parted but the shadow with his hand.

What! was it you that would be England's king?

Was it you that revelled in our parliament and made a preachment of your high descent?

Where are your mess of sons to back you now?

The wanton Edward, and the lusty George?

And where's that valiant crook-back prodigy, Dicky your boy, that with his grumbling voice was wont to cheer his dad in mutinies?

Or, with the rest, where is your darling Rutland?

Look, York, I stained this napkin with the blood that valiant Clifford, with his rapier's point, made issue from the bosom of the boy

If thine eyes can water for his death, I give thee this to dry thy cheeks withal.

Alas poor York! but that I hate thee deadly, I should lament thy miserable state.

I pray to thee, grieve to make me merry York.

What hath thy fiery heart so parched thine entrails that not a tear can fall for Rutland's death?

Why art thou patient, man? thou shouldst be mad

I, to make thee mad, do mock thee thus.

Stamp, rave, and fret, that I may sing and dance.

Thou wouldst be feed, I see, to make me sport, York cannot speak, unless he wear a crown.

A crown for York! and, lords, bow low to him, hold you his hands whilst I do set it on.

(Putting a paper crown on his head)

Ay marry sir, now looks he like a king!

Ay, this is he that took King Henry's chair and this is he was his adopted heir.

But how is it that great Plantagenet is crowned so soon and broke his solemn oath?

As I bethink me, you should not be king till our King Henry had shook hands with death, and will you pale your head in Henry's glory, rob his temples of the diadem, now in his life against your holy oath?

Oh it is a fault too too unpardonable!

Off with the crown, and with the crown his head

Whilst we breathe, take time to do him dead.

Clifford

That is my office, for my father's sake.

Queen Margaret

Nay, stay

Lets hear the orisons he makes.

York

She-wolf of France, but worse than wolves of France, whose tongue more poisons than the adder's tooth!

How ill-beseeming is it in thy sex to triumph like an Amazonian trull upon their woes whom fortune captivates!

But that thy face is, vizard-like, unchanging, made impudent with use of evil deeds, I would assay, proud queen, to make thee blush.

To tell thee whence thou camest, of whom derived, were shame enough to shame thee, wert thou not shameless.

Thy father bears the type of King of Naples of both the Sicils and Jerusalem, yet not so wealthy as an English yeoman.

Hath that poor monarch taught thee to insult?

It needs not, nor it boots thee not, proud queen, unless the adage must be verified, that beggars mounted run their horse to death.

It is beauty that doth oft make women proud

God he knows, thy share thereof is small, it is virtue that doth make them most admired

The contrary doth make thee wondered at, it is government that makes them seem divine

The want thereof makes thee abominable, thou art as opposite to every good as the Antipodes are unto us, or as the south to the septentrion.

Oh tiger's heart wrapt in a woman's hide!

How couldst thou drain the life-blood of the child, to bid the father wipe his eyes withal and yet be seen to bear a woman's face?

Women are soft, mild, pitiful and flexible

Thou stern, obdurate, flinty, rough, remorseless.

Bids't thou me rage? why, now thou hast thy wish, wouldst have me weep?

Why, now thou hast thy will, for raging wind blows up incessant showers and when the rage allays, the rain begins.

These tears are my sweet Rutland's obsequies, and every drop cries vengeance for his death, against thee, fell Clifford, and thee, false Frenchwoman.

Northumberland

Beshrew me, but his passion moves me so that hardly can I cheque my eyes from tears.

York

That face of his the hungry cannibals would not have touched, would not have stained with blood, but you are more inhuman, more inexorable, oh ten times more than tigers of Hyrcania.

See, ruthless queen, a hapless father's tears, this cloth thou dip'dst in blood of my sweet boy and I with tears do wash the blood away.

Keep thou the napkin, and go boast of this, and if thou tell'st the heavy story right, upon my soul, the hearers will shed tears.

Yea even my foes will shed fast-falling tears and say alas, it was a piteous deed!

There, take the crown, and, with the crown, my curse

In thy need such comfort come to thee as now I reap at thy too cruel hand!

Hard-hearted Clifford, take me from the world,

my soul to heaven, my blood upon your heads!

Northumberland

Had he been slaughter-man to all my kin, I should not for my life but weep with him.

To see how inly sorrow gripes his soul.

Queen Margaret

What, weeping-ripe, my Lord Northumberland?

Think but upon the wrong he did us all and that will quickly dry thy melting tears.

Clifford

Here's for my oath, here's for my father's death.

(Stabbing him)

Queen Margaret

And here's to right our gentle-hearted king.

(Stabbing him)

York

Open Thy gate of mercy, gracious God!

My soul flies through these wounds to seek out thee.

(Dies)

Queen Margaret

Off with his head, and set it on York gates

So York may overlook the town of York.

(Flourish)

(Exit)

Act 2 Scene 1

A plain near Mortimer's Cross in Herefordshire.

(Edward, Richard, and their power enter marching)

Edward

I wonder how our princely father escaped, or whether he be escaped away or no from Clifford's and Northumberland's pursuit, had he been taken, we should have heard the news

Had he been slain, we should have heard the news

Had he escaped, methinks we should have heard the happy tidings of his good escape.

How fares my brother? why is he so sad?

Richard

I cannot joy, until I be resolved where our right valiant father is become.

I saw him in the battle range about

Watched him how he singled Clifford forth.

Methought he bore him in the thickest troop as doth a lion in a herd of neat

As a bear, encompassed round with dogs, who having pinched a few and made them cry, the rest stand all aloof, and bark at him.

So fared our father with his enemies

So fled his enemies my warlike father, methinks, it is prize enough to be his son.

See how the morning opens her golden gates and takes her farewell of the glorious sun!

How well resembles it the prime of youth trimmed like a younker prancing to his love!

Edward

Dazzle mine eyes, or do I see three suns?

Richard

Three glorious suns, each one a perfect sun

Not separated with the racking clouds but severed in a pale clear-shining sky.

See, see! they join, embrace, and seem to kiss, as if they vowed some league inviolable, now are they but one lamp, one light, one sun.

In this the heaven figures some event.

Edward

It is wondrous strange, the like yet never heard of.

I think it cites us brother, to the field that we, the sons of brave Plantagenet, each one already blazing by our meeds should notwithstanding join our lights together and over-shine the earth as this the world.

Whate'er it bodes, henceforward will I bear upon my target three fair-shining suns.

Richard

Nay, bear three daughters: by your leave I speak it, you love the breeder better than the male.

(A Messenger enters)

But what art thou, whose heavy looks foretell some dreadful story hanging on thy tongue?

Messenger

Ah, one that was a woeful looker-on when as the noble Duke of York was slain, your princely father and my loving lord!

Edward

Oh speak no more, for I have heard too much.

Richard

Say how he died, for I will hear it all.

Messenger

Environed he was with many foes and stood against them, as the hope of Troy against the Greeks that would have entered Troy.

But Hercules himself must yield to odds

Many strokes, though with a little axe, chew down and fell the hardest-timber'd oak.

By many hands your father was subdued

Only slaughtered by the ireful arm of unrelenting Clifford and the queen, who crowned the gracious duke in high despite, laughs in his face

When with grief he wept, the ruthless queen gave him to dry his cheeks a napkin steeped in the harmless blood of sweet young Rutland, by rough Clifford slain, and after many scorns, many foul taunts, they took his head and on the gates of York they set the same

There it doth remain the saddest spectacle that ever I viewed.

Edward

Sweet Duke of York, our prop to lean upon, now thou art gone, we have no staff, no stay.

Oh Clifford, boisterous Clifford! thou hast slain the flower of Europe for his chivalry

Treacherously hast thou vanquished him, for hand to hand he would have vanquished thee.

Now my soul's palace is become a prison, ah, would she break from hence, that this my body might in the ground be closed up in rest!

For never henceforth shall I joy again, never oh never shall I see more joy!

Richard

I cannot weep; for all my body's moisture scarce serves to quench my furnace-burning heart, nor can my tongue unload my heart's great burthen

For selfsame wind that I should speak withal is kindling coals that fires all my breast and burns me up with flames that tears would quench.

To weep is to make less the depth of grief, tears then for babes; blows and revenge for me Richard, I bear thy name

I'll venge thy death, or die renowned by attempting it.

Edward

His name that valiant duke hath left with thee

His dukedom and his chair with me is left.

Richard

Nay, if thou be that princely eagle's bird, show thy descent by gazing against the sun, for chair and dukedom, throne and kingdom say

Either that is thine, or else thou wert not his.

(Warwick, Montague, and their army enter, marching)

Warwick

How now, fair lords! What fare? what news abroad?

Richard

Great Lord of Warwick, if we should recount our baleful news, and at each word's deliverance stab poniards in our flesh till all were told the words would add more anguish than the wounds.

Oh valiant lord, the Duke of York is slain!

Edward

Oh Warwick, Warwick! that Plantagenet, which held three dearly as his soul's redemption, is by the stern Lord Clifford done to death.

Warwick

Ten days ago I drowned these news in tears

Now, to add more measure to your woes, I come to tell you things sit here then befallen.

After the bloody fray at Wakefield fought, where your brave father breathed his latest gasp tidings, as swiftly as the posts could run, were brought me of your loss and his depart.

I, then in London keeper of the king, mustered my soldiers, gathered flocks of friends and very well appointed, as I thought, marched toward Saint Alban's to intercept the queen, bearing the king in my behalf along

For by my scouts I was advertised that she was coming with a full intent to dash our late decree in parliament touching King Henry's oath and your succession.

Short tale to make, we at Saint Alban's met our battles join'd, and both sides fiercely fought, but whether it was the coldness of the king,

Who looked full gently on his warlike queen, that robbed my soldiers of their heated spleen

Or whether it was report of her success

Or more than common fear of Clifford's rigour, who thunders to his captives blood and death, I cannot judge: but to conclude with truth, their weapons like to lightning came and went

Our soldiers', like the night-owl's lazy flight, or like an idle thresher with a flail, fell gently down as if they struck their friends.

I cheered them up with justice of our cause, with promise of high pay and great rewards, but all in vain

They had no heart to fight and we in them no hope to win the day

So that we fled; the king unto the queen

Lord George your brother, Norfolk and myself, in haste, post-haste, are come to join with you, for in the marches here we heard you were making another head to fight again.

Edward

Where is the Duke of Norfolk, gentle Warwick?

And when came George from Burgundy to England?

Warwick

Some six miles off the duke is with the soldiers

For your brother, he was lately sent from your kind aunt, Duchess of Burgundy with aid of soldiers to this needful war.

Richard

It was odds, belike, when valiant Warwick fled, often have I heard his praises in pursuit, but never till now his scandal of retire.

Warwick

Nor now my scandal, Richard, dost thou hear

For thou shalt know this strong right hand of mine can pluck the diadem from faint Henry's head, and wring the awful sceptre from his fist, were he as famous and as bold in war as he is famed for mildness, peace, and prayer.

Richard

I know it well, Lord Warwick; blame me not, it is love I bear thy glories makes me speak.

But in this troublous time what's to be done?

Shall we go throw away our coats of steel, and wrap our bodies in black mourning gowns, numbering our Ave-Maries with our beads?

Or shall we on the helmets of our foes tell our devotion with revengeful arms?

If for the last, say ay, and to it lords.

Warwick

Why, therefore Warwick came to seek you out

Therefore comes my brother Montague.

Attend me, lords.

The proud insulting queen, with Clifford and the naught Northumberland and of their feather many more proud birds have wrought the easy-melting king like wax.

He swore consent to your succession, his oath enrolled in the parliament

Now to London all the crew are gone, to frustrate both his oath and what beside may make against the house of Lancaster.

Their power, I think, is thirty thousand strong

Now, if the help of Norfolk and myself, with all the friends that thou brave Earl of March, amongst the loving Welshmen canst procure, will but amount to five and twenty thousand

Why, Via! to London will we march with hands and once again bestride our foaming steeds and once again cry Charge upon our foes!

But never once again turn back and fly.

Richard

Ay, now methinks I hear great Warwick speak, never may he live to see a sunshine day, that cries Retire, if Warwick bid him stay.

Edward

Lord Warwick, on thy shoulder will I lean

When thou fail'st...

As God forbid the hour!...

Must Edward fall, which peril heaven forfend!

Warwick

No longer Earl of March, but Duke of York, the next degree is England's royal throne

For King of England shalt thou be proclaimed in every borough as we pass along

He that throws not up his cap for joy shall for the fault make forfeit of his head.

King Edward, valiant Richard, Montague, stay we no longer dreaming of renown, but sound the trumpets, and about our task.

Richard

Then, Clifford, were thy heart as hard as steel, as thou hast shown it flinty by thy deeds, I come to pierce it, or to give thee mine.

Edward

Then strike up drums: God and Saint George for us!

(A Messenger enters)

Warwick

How now! what news?

Messenger

The Duke of Norfolk sends you word by me, the queen is coming with a puissant host, craves your company for speedy counsel.

Warwick

Why then it sorts, brave warriors, let's away.

(Exit)

Act 2 Scene 2

Before York.

Flourish

(King Henry VI, Queen Margaret, Prince Edward, Clifford, and Northumberland, with drum and trumpets enter)

Queen Margaret

Welcome, my lord, to this brave town of York.

Yonder's the head of that arch-enemy that sought to be encompassed with your crown, doth not the object cheer your heart, my lord?

King Henry VI

Ay, as the rocks cheer them that fear their wreck, to see this sight, it irks my very soul.

Withhold revenge, dear God! It is not my fault, nor wittingly have I infringed my vow.

Clifford

My gracious liege, this too much lenity and harmful pity must be laid aside.

To whom do lions cast their gentle looks?

Not to the beast that would usurp their den.

Whose hand is that the forest bear doth lick?

Not his that spoils her young before her face.

Who escapes the lurking serpent's mortal sting?

Not he that sets his foot upon her back.

The smallest worm will turn being trodden on, and Jupiter will peck in safeguard of their brood.

Ambitious York doth level at thy crown, thou smiling while he knit his angry brows, he, but a duke would have his son a king and raise his issue like a loving sire

Thou, being a king, blest with a goodly son, didst yield consent to disinherit him, which argued thee a most unloving father.

Unreasonable creatures feed their young and though man's face be fearful to their eyes, yet in protection of their tender ones who hath not seen them, even with those wings which sometime they have used with fearful flight make war with him that climbed unto their nest offer their own lives in their young's defence?

For shame, my liege, make them your precedent!

Were it not pity that this goodly boy should lose his birthright by his father's fault and long hereafter say unto his child, what my great-grandfather and his grandsire got my careless father fondly gave away?

Ah, what a shame were this! Look on the boy

Let his manly face, which promiseth successful fortune, steel thy melting heart to hold thine own and leave thine own with him.

King Henry VI

Full well hath Clifford played the orator, inferring arguments of mighty force.

Clifford, tell me, didst thou never hear that things ill-got had ever bad success?

And happy always was it for that son whose father for his hoarding went to hell?

I'll leave my son my virtuous deeds behind

Would my father had left me no more!

For all the rest is held at such a rate as brings a thousand-fold more care to keep than in possession and jot of pleasure.

Ah, cousin York! would thy best friends did know how it doth grieve me that thy head is here!

Queen Margaret

My lord, cheer up your spirits, our foes are nigh, and this soft courage makes your followers faint.

You promised knighthood to our forward son, unsheathe your sword, and dub him presently.

(Edward, kneel down)

King Henry VI

Edward Plantagenet, arise a knight

Learn this lesson, draw thy sword in right.

Prince

My gracious father, by your kingly leave, I'll draw it as apparent to the crown and in that quarrel use it to the death.

Clifford

Why, that is spoken like a toward prince.

(A Messenger enters)

Messenger

Royal commanders, be in readiness, for with a band of thirty thousand men comes Warwick, backing of the Duke of York

In the towns, as they do march along proclaims him king, and many fly to him, during your battle, for they are at hand.

Clifford

I would your highness would depart the field, the queen hath best success when you are absent.

Queen Margaret

Ay, good my lord, and leave us to our fortune.

King Henry VI

Why, that's my fortune too; therefore I'll stay.

Northumberland

Be it with resolution then to fight.

Prince Edward

My royal father, cheer these noble lords and hearten those that fight in your defence, unsheathe your sword, good father

(Cries Saint George!)

(Edward, George, Richard, Warwick, Norfolk, Montague, and Soldiers enter marching)

Edward

Now, perjured Henry! wilt thou kneel for grace and set thy diadem upon my head

Or bide the mortal fortune of the field?

Queen Margaret

Go, rate thy minions, proud insulting boy!

Becomes it thee to be thus bold in terms before thy sovereign and thy lawful king?

Edward

I am his king, and he should bow his knee

I was adopted heir by his consent, since when his oath is broke

As I hear, you, that are king, though he do wear the crown, have caused him, by new act of parliament to blot out me, and put his own son in.

Clifford

And reason too, who should succeed the father but the son?

Richard

Are you there, butcher?

Oh, I cannot speak!

Clifford

Ay, crook-back, here I stand to answer thee, or any he the proudest of thy sort.

Richard

It was you that killed young Rutland, was it not?

Clifford

Ay, and old York, and yet not satisfied.

Richard

For God's sake, lords, give signal to the fight.

Warwick

What say'st thou, Henry, wilt thou yield the crown?

Queen Margaret

Why, how now, long-tongued Warwick! dare you speak?

When you and I met at Saint Alban's last,

Your legs did better service than your hands.

Warwick

Then 'twas my turn to fly, and now 'tis thine.

Clifford

You said so much before, and yet you fled.

Warwick

It was not your valour, Clifford, drove me thence.

Northumberland

No, nor your manhood that durst make you stay.

Richard

Northumberland, I hold thee reverently.

Break off the parley; for scarce I can refrain the execution of my big-swollen heart upon that Clifford, that cruel child-killer.

Clifford

I slew thy father, call'st thou him a child?

Richard

Ay, like a dastard and a treacherous coward, as thou didst kill our tender brother Rutland

Were sunset I'll make thee curse the deed.

King Henry VI

Have done with words, my lords, and hear me speak.

Queen Margaret

Defy them then, or else hold close thy lips.

King Henry VI

I pray I to thee, give no limits to my tongue, I am a king, and privileged to speak.

Clifford

My liege, the wound that bred this meeting here cannot be cured by words; therefore be still.

Richard

Then, executioner, unsheathe thy sword, by him that made us all, I am resolved that Clifford's manhood lies upon his tongue.

Edward

Say, Henry, shall I have my right, or no?

A thousand men have broke their fasts to-day that never shall dine unless thou yield the crown.

Warwick

If thou deny, their blood upon thy head

For York in justice puts his armour on.

Prince Edward

If that be right which Warwick says is right, there is no wrong, but everything is right.

Richard

Whoever got thee, there thy mother stands

Well I wot, thou hast thy mother's tongue.

Queen Margaret

But thou art neither like thy sire nor dam

Like a foul mis-shapen stigmatic, marked by the destinies to be avoided as venom toads, or lizards' dreadful stings.

Richard

Iron of Naples hid with English gilt whose father bears the title of a king...

As if a channel should be called the sea...

Shamest thou not, knowing whence thou art extraught to let thy tongue detect thy base-born heart?

Edward

A wisp of straw were worth a thousand crowns to make this shameless callet know herself.

Helen of Greece was fairer far than thou, although thy husband may be Menelaus

Never was Agamemnon's brother wronged by that false woman, as this king by thee.

His father revelled in the heart of France and tamed the king, and made the dauphin stoop

Had he matched according to his state, he might have kept that glory to this day

When he took a beggar to his bed and graced thy poor sire with his bridal-day, even then that sunshine brewed a shower for him that washed his father's fortunes forth of France, and heaped sedition on his crown at home.

For what hath broached this tumult but thy pride?

Hadst thou been meek, our title still had slept

We, in pity of the gentle king, had slipped our claim until another age.

George

But when we saw our sunshine made thy spring and that thy summer bred us no increase, we set the axe to thy usurping root

Though the edge hath something hit ourselves, yet, know thou, since we have begun to strike, we'll never leave till we have hewn thee down or bathed thy growing with our heated bloods.

Edward

And, in this resolution, I defy thee

Not willing any longer conference since thou deniest the gentle king to speak.

Sound trumpets! let our bloody colours wave!

And either victory, or else a grave.

Queen Margaret

Stay, Edward.

Edward

No, wrangling woman, we'll no longer stay:

These words will cost ten thousand lives this day.

(Exit)

Act 2 Scene 3

A field of battle between Towton and Saxton, in Yorkshire.

(Alarum)

(Excursions)

(Warwick enters)

Warwick

Forspent with toil, as runners with a race, I lay me down a little while to breathe

Strokes received, many blows repaid have robbed my strong-knit sinews of their strength, and spite of spite needs must I rest awhile.

(Edward enters running)

Edward

Smile, gentle heaven! or strike, ungentle death!

For this world frowns and Edward's sun is clouded.

Warwick

How now, my lord! what hap? what hope of good?

(George enters)

George

Our hap is loss, our hope but sad despair

Our ranks are broke, and ruin follows us, what counsel give you? Whither shall we fly?

Edward

Bootless is flight, they follow us with wings

Weak we are and cannot shun pursuit.

(Richard enters)

Richard

Ah, Warwick, why hast thou withdrawn thyself?

Thy brother's blood the thirsty earth hath drunk,

Broached with the steely point of Clifford's lance

In the very pangs of death he cried, like to a dismal clangour heard from afar, Warwick, revenge! brother, revenge my death!

So, underneath the belly of their steeds that stained their fetlocks in his smoking blood, the noble gentleman gave up the ghost.

Warwick

Then let the earth be drunken with our blood, I'll kill my horse, because I will not fly.

Why stand we like soft-hearted women here, wailing our losses whiles the foe doth rage

Look upon, as if the tragedy were played in jest by counterfeiting actors?

Here on my knee I vow to God above, I'll never pause again, never stand still till either death hath closed these eyes of mine or fortune given me measure of revenge.

Edward

Oh Warwick, I do bend my knee with thine

In this vow do chain my soul to thine!

And here my knee rise from the earth's cold face, I throw my hands, mine eyes, my heart to thee

Thou setter up and plucker down of kings, beseeching thee, if with they will it stands that to my foes this body must be prey, yet that thy brazen gates of heaven may open and give sweet passage to my sinful soul!

Now, lords, take leave until we meet again, wherever it be, in heaven or in earth.

Richard

Brother, give me thy hand; and, gentle Warwick, let me embrace thee in my weary arms, I, that did never weep, now melt with woe that winter should cut off our spring-time so.

Warwick

Away, away! Once more, sweet lords farewell.

George

Yet let us all together to our troops and give them leave to fly that will not stay

Call them pillars that will stand to us

If we thrive, promise them such rewards as victors wear at the Olympian games, this may plant courage in their quailing breasts

Yet is hope of life and victory.

Forslow no longer, make we hence amain.

(Exit)

Act 2 Scene 4

Another part of the field.

(Excursions)

(Richard and Clifford enters)

Richard

Now, Clifford, I have singled thee alone, suppose this arm is for the Duke of York, and this for Rutland, both bound to revenge wert thou environed with a brazen wall.

Clifford

Now, Richard, I am with thee here alone, this is the hand that stabbed thy father York

This the hand that slew thy brother Rutland, here's the heart that triumphs in their death and cheers these hands that slew thy sire, and brother to execute the like upon thyself

So, have at thee!

(Clifford and Richard fight, Warwick comes, Clifford flies)

Richard

Nay Warwick, single out some other chase

I myself will hunt this wolf to death.

(Exit)

Act 2 Scene 5

Another part of the field.

(Alarum)

(King Henry VI enters alone)

King Henry VI

This battle fares like to the morning's war when dying clouds contend with growing light, what time the shepherd, blowing of his nails, can neither call it perfect day nor night.

Now sways it this way, like a mighty sea forced by the tide to combat with the wind

Now sways it that way like the selfsame sea forced to retire by fury of the wind, sometime the flood prevails, and then the wind

Now one the better, then another best

Both tugging to be victors, breast to breast, yet neither conqueror nor conquered, so is the equal of this fell war.

Here on this molehill will I sit me down.

To whom God will, there be the victory!

For Margaret my queen, and Clifford too have chid me from the battle

Swearing both they prosper best of all when I am thence.

Would I were dead! if God's good will were so

What is in this world but grief and woe?

Oh God! methinks it were a happy life, to be no better than a homely swain

To sit upon a hill, as I do now, to carve out dials quaintly, point by point, thereby to see the minutes how they run

How many make the hour full complete

How many hours bring about the day

How many days will finish up the year

How many years a mortal man may live.

When this is known, then to divide the times, so many hours must I tend my flock

So many hours must I take my rest

So many hours must I contemplate

So many hours must I sport myself

So many days my ewes have been with young

So many weeks ere the poor fools will yean, so many years were I shall shear the fleece, so minutes, hours, days, months, and years passed over to the end they were created would bring white hairs unto a quiet grave.

Ah, what a life were this! how sweet! how lovely!

Gives not the hawthorn-bush a sweeter shade to shepherds looking on their silly sheep, than doth a rich embroidered canopy to kings that fear their subjects' treachery?

Oh, yes, it doth

A thousand-fold it doth.

And to conclude, the shepherd's homely curds his cold thin drink out of his leather bottle.

His wonted sleep under a fresh tree's shade, all which secure and sweetly he enjoys, is far beyond a prince's delicates, his viands sparkling in a golden cup, his body couched in a curious bed when care, mistrust, and treason waits on him.

(Alarum)

(A Son that has killed his father enters, dragging in the dead body)

Son

Ill blows the wind that profits nobody.

This man, whom hand to hand I slew in fight may be possessed with some store of crowns, that haply take them from him now may yet were night yield both my life and them

To some man else, as this dead man doth me.

Who's this? Oh God!

It is my father's face whom in this conflict I unwares have killed.

Oh heavy times, begetting such events!

From London by the king was I pressed forth

My father, being the Earl of Warwick's man came on the part of York, pressed by his master and I, who at his hands received my life, him have by my hands of life bereaved him.

Pardon me, God, I knew not what I did!

And pardon, father, for I knew not thee!

My tears shall wipe away these bloody marks

No more words till they have flowed their fill.

King Henry VI

Oh piteous spectacle! Oh bloody times!

Whiles lions war and battle for their dens, poor harmless lambs abide their enmity.

Weep, wretched man, I'll aid thee tear for tear

Let our hearts and eyes, like civil war, be blind with tears and break overcharged with grief.

(A Father that has killed his son enters, bringing in the body)

Father

Thou that so stoutly hast resisted me, give me thy gold, if thou hast any gold for I have bought it with an hundred blows.

But let me see: is this our foeman's face?

Ah, no, no, no, it is mine only son!

Ah, boy, if any life be left in thee, throw up thine eye! see, see what showers arise blown with the windy tempest of my heart

Upon thy words, that kill mine eye and heart!

Oh, pity, God, this miserable age!

What stratagems, how fell, how butcherly, erroneous, mutinous and unnatural, this deadly quarrel daily doth beget!

Oh boy, thy father gave thee life too soon and hath bereft thee of thy life too late!

King Henry VI

Woe above woe! grief more than common grief!

Oh that my death would stay these ruthful deeds!

Oh pity, pity, gentle heaven, pity!

The red rose and the white are on his face, the fatal colours of our striving houses, the one his purple blood right well resembles

The other his pale cheeks, methinks, presenteth, wither one rose and let the other flourish

If you contend, a thousand lives must wither.

Son

How will my mother for a father's death take on with me and never be satisfied!

Father

How will my wife for slaughter of my son shed seas of tears and ne'er be satisfied!

King Henry VI

How will the country for these woful chances methinks the king and not be satisfied!

Son

Was ever son so rued a father's death?

Father

Was ever father so bemoaned his son?

King Henry VI

Was ever king so grieved for subjects' woe?

Much is your sorrow; mine ten times so much.

Son

I'll bear thee hence, where I may weep my fill.

(Exits with the body)

Father

These arms of mine shall be thy winding-sheet

My heart, sweet boy, shall be thy sepulchre, for from my heart thine image ne'er shall go

My sighing breast shall be thy funeral bell and so obsequious will thy father be, even for the loss of thee, having no more as Priam was for all his valiant sons.

I'll bear thee hence; and let them fight that will, for I have murdered where I should not kill.

(Exits with the body)

King Henry VI

Sad-hearted men, much overgone with care, here sits a king more woful than you are.

(Alarums)

(Excursions)

(Queen Margaret, Prince Edward, and Exeter enter)

Prince Edward

Fly, father, fly! for all your friends are fled and Warwick rages like a chafed bull away!

For death doth hold us in pursuit.

Queen Margaret

Mount you, my lord; towards Berwick post amain, Edward and Richard, like a brace of greyhounds having the fearful flying hare in sight with fiery eyes sparkling for very wrath and bloody steel grasped in their ireful hands are at our backs

Therefore hence amain.

Exeter

Away! for vengeance comes along with them, nay, stay not to expostulate, make speed

Or else come after, I'll away before.

King Henry VI

Nay, take me with thee, good sweet Exeter, not that I fear to stay, but love to go whither the queen intends. Forward

Away!

(Exit)

Act 2 Scene 6

Another part of the field.

A loud alarum.

(Clifford enters wounded)

Clifford

Here burns my candle out

Ay, here it dies which whiles it lasted gave King Henry light.

Oh Lancaster, I fear thy overthrow more than my body's parting with my soul!

My love and fear glued many friends to thee

Now I fall, thy tough commixture melts.

Impairing Henry, strengthening misproud York, the common people swarm like summer flies

And whither fly the gnats but to the sun?

And who shines now but Henry's enemies?

Oh Phoebus, hadst thou never given consent that Phaethon should cheque thy fiery steeds, thy burning car never had scorched the earth!

And, Henry, hadst thou swayed as kings should do, or as thy father and his father did, giving no ground unto the house of York they never then had sprung like summer flies

I and ten thousand in this luckless realm had left no mourning widows for our death

Thou this day hadst kept thy chair in peace.

For what doth cherish weeds but gentle air?

And what makes robbers bold but too much lenity?

Bootless are plaints, and cureless are my wounds

No way to fly, nor strength to hold out flight, the foe is merciless, and will not pity

For at their hands I have deserved no pity.

The air hath got into my deadly wounds and much effuse of blood doth make me faint.

Come, York and Richard, Warwick and the rest

I stabbed your fathers' bosoms, split my breast.

(He faints)

Alarum and retreat)

(Edward, George, Richard, Montague, Warwick, and Soldiers enters)

Edward

Now breathe we, lords: good fortune bids us pause and smooth the frowns of war with peaceful looks.

Some troops pursue the bloody-minded queen, that led calm Henry, though he were a king as doth a sail, filled with a fretting gust command an argosy to stem the waves.

But think you, lords, that Clifford fled with them?

Warwick

No, it is impossible he should escape, for, though before his face I speak the words your brother Richard marked him for the grave, and wheresoever he is, he's surely dead.

(Clifford groans, and dies)

Edward

Whose soul is that which takes her heavy leave?

Richard

A deadly groan, like life and death's departing.

Edward

See who it is, and now the battle's ended, if friend or foe let him be gently used.

Richard

Revoke that doom of mercy, for 'tis Clifford

Who not contented that he lopped the branch in chewing Rutland when his leaves put forth, but set his murdering knife unto the root from whence that tender spray did sweetly spring, I mean our princely father, Duke of York.

Warwick

From off the gates of York fetch down the head, your father's head, which Clifford placed there

Instead whereof let this supply the room, measure for measure must be answered.

Edward

Bring forth that fatal screech-owl to our house, that nothing sung but death to us and ours, now death shall stop his dismal threatening sound and his ill-boding tongue no more shall speak.

Warwick

I think his understanding is bereft.

Speak, Clifford, dost thou know who speaks to thee?

Dark cloudy death overshades his beams of life and he nor sees nor hears us what we say.

Richard

Oh, would he did! and so perhaps he doth, it is but his policy to counterfeit, because he would avoid such bitter taunts which in the time of death he gave our father.

George

If so thou think'st, vex him with eager words.

Richard

Clifford, ask mercy and obtain no grace.

Edward

Clifford, repent in bootless penitence.

Warwick

Clifford, devise excuses for thy faults.

George

While we devise fell tortures for thy faults.

Richard

Thou didst love York, and I am son to York.

Edward

Thou pitied'st Rutland

I will pity thee.

George

Where's Captain Margaret, to fence you now?

Warwick

They mock thee, Clifford: swear as thou wast wont.

Richard

What, not an oath? nay, then the world goes hard when Clifford cannot spare his friends an oath.

I know by that he's dead; and, by my soul, if this right hand would buy two hour's life that I in all despite might rail at him

This hand should chop it off, and with the issuing blood stifle the villain whose unstanched thirst York and young Rutland could not satisfy.

Warwick

Ay, but he's dead: off with the traitor's head and rear it in the place your father's stands.

And now to London with triumphant march, there to be crowned England's royal king, from whence shall Warwick cut the sea to France and ask the Lady Bona for thy queen

So shalt thou sinew both these lands together, and having France thy friend, thou shalt not dread the scattered foe that hopes to rise again

For though they cannot greatly sting to hurt, yet look to have them buzz to offend thine ears.

First will I see the coronation

Then to Brittany I'll cross the sea, to effect this marriage, so it please my lord.

Edward

Even as thou wilt, sweet Warwick, let it be

For in thy shoulder do I build my seat and never will I undertake the thing wherein thy counsel and consent is wanting.

Richard, I will create thee Duke of Gloucester and George, of Clarence: Warwick, as ourself shall do and undo as him pleaseth best.

Richard

Let me be Duke of Clarence, George of Gloucester

For Gloucester's dukedom is too ominous.

Warwick

Tut, that's a foolish observation, Richard, be Duke of Gloucester.

Now to London to see these honours in possession.

Exit

Act 3 Scene 1

A forest in the north of England.

(Two Keepers enter with cross-bows in their hands)

First Keeper

Under this thick-grown brake we'll shroud ourselves

For through this laund anon the deer will come

In this covert will we make our stand, culling the principal of all the deer.

Second Keeper

I'll stay above the hill, so both may shoot.

First Keeper

That cannot be

The noise of thy cross-bow will scare the herd, and so my shoot is lost.

Here stand we both, and aim we at the best, and for the time shall not seem tedious, I'll tell thee what befell me on a day in this self-place where now we mean to stand.

Second Keeper

Here comes a man; let's stay till he be past.

(King Henry VI enters disguised, with a prayerbook)

King Henry VI

From Scotland am I stollen, even of pure love, to greet mine own land with my wishful sight.

No, Harry, Harry, it is no land of thine

Thy place is filled, thy sceptre wrung from thee, thy balm washed off wherewith thou was it anointed, no bending knee will call thee Caesar now

No humble suitors press to speak for right, no, not a man comes for redress of thee

For how can I help them, and not myself?

First Keeper

Ay, here's a deer whose skin's a keeper's fee, this is the quondam king; let's seize upon him.

King Henry VI

Let me embrace thee, sour adversity, for wise men say it is the wisest course.

Second Keeper

Why linger we? Let us lay hands upon him.

First Keeper

Forbear awhile

We'll hear a little more.

King Henry VI

My queen and son are gone to France for aid, and as I hear the great commanding Warwick is thither gone to crave the French king's sister, to wife for Edward

If this news be true, poor queen and son, your labour is but lost

For Warwick is a subtle orator and Lewis a prince soon won with moving words, by this account then Margaret may win him

For she's a woman to be pitied much, her sighs will make a battery in his breast

Her tears will pierce into a marble heart

The tiger will be mild whiles she doth mourn

Nero will be tainted with remorse to hear and see her plaints, her brinish tears.

Ay, but she's come to beg, Warwick to give

She, on his left side, craving aid for Henry, he, on his right asking a wife for Edward

She weeps, and says her Henry is deposed

He smiles, and says his Edward is installed

That she, poor wretch, for grief can speak no more

Whiles Warwick tells his title, smooths the wrong, inferreth arguments of mighty strength and in conclusion wins the king from her with promise of his sister, and what else to strengthen and support King Edward's place.

Oh Margaret, thus it will be, and thou, poor soul,aArt then forsaken, as thou went'st forlorn!

Second Keeper

Say, what art thou that talk'st of kings and queens?

King Henry VI

More than I seem, and less than I was born to, a man at least, for less I should not be

And men may talk of kings, and why not I?

Second Keeper

Ay, but thou talk'st as if thou wert a king.

King Henry VI

Why, so I am, in mind

That's enough.

Second Keeper

But, if thou be a king, where is thy crown?

King Henry VI

My crown is in my heart, not on my head

Not decked with diamonds and Indian stones, nor to be seen: my crown is called content, a crown it is that seldom kings enjoy.

Second Keeper

Well, if you be a king crowned with content, your crown content and you must be contented to go along with us

For as we think, you are the king King Edward hath deposed we his subjects sworn in all allegiance and will apprehend you as his enemy.

King Henry VI

But did you never swear, and break an oath?

Second Keeper

No, never such an oath; nor will not now.

King Henry VI

Where did you dwell when I was King of England?

Second Keeper

Here in this country, where we now remain.

King Henry VI

I was anointed king at nine months old

My father and my grandfather were kings and you were sworn true subjects unto me, and tell me then, have you not broke your oaths?

First Keeper

No

For we were subjects but while you were king.

King Henry VI

Why, am I dead? do I not breathe a man?

Ah, simple men, you know not what you swear!

Look, as I blow this feather from my face and as the air blows it to me again, obeying with my wind when I do blow and yielding to another when it blows, commanded always by the greater gust

Such is the lightness of you common men.

But do not break your oaths

For of that sin my mild entreaty shall not make you guilty.

Go where you will, the king shall be commanded

Be you kings, command, and I'll obey.

First Keeper

We are true subjects to the king, King Edward.

King Henry VI

So would you be again to Henry, if he were seated as King Edward is.

First Keeper

We charge you, in God's name, and the king's to go with us unto the officers.

King Henry VI

In God's name, lead; your king's name be obeyed, and what God will, that let your king perform

What he will, I humbly yield unto.

(Exit)

Act 3 Scene 2

London. The palace.

(King Edward IV, Gloucester, Clarence, and Lady Grey enter)

King Edward IV

Brother of Gloucester, at Saint Alban's field this lady's husband, Sir Richard Grey was slain, his lands then seized on by the conqueror, her suit is now to repossess those lands

Which we in justice cannot well deny because in quarrel of the house of York the worthy gentleman did lose his life

Gloucester

Your highness shall do well to grant her suit

It were dishonour to deny it her.

King Edward IV

It were no less

Yet I'll make a pause.

Gloucester

(From Aside to Clarence) Yea, is it so?

I see the lady hath a thing to grant before the king will grant her humble suit.

Clarence

(From Aside to Gloucester) He knows the game, how true he keeps the wind!

Gloucester

(From Aside to Clarence) Silence!

King Edward IV

Widow, we will consider of your suit

Come some other time to know our mind.

Lady Grey

Right gracious lord, I cannot brook delay, may it please your highness to resolve me now

What your pleasure is, shall satisfy me.

Gloucester

(From Aside to Clarence) Ay, widow? then I'll warrant you all your lands,

And if what pleases him shall pleasure you.

Fight closer, or, good faith, you'll catch a blow.

Clarence

(From Aside to Gloucester) I fear her not, unless she chance to fall.

Gloucester

(From Aside to Clarence) God forbid that! for he'll take vantages.

King Edward IV

How many children hast thou, widow? tell me.

Clarence

(From Aside to Gloucester) I think he means to beg a child of her.

Gloucester

(From Aside to Clarence) Nay, whip me then, he'll rather give her two.

Lady Grey

Three, my most gracious lord.

Gloucester

(From Aside to Clarence) You shall have four, if you'll be ruled by him.

King Edward IV

It were pity they should lose their father's lands.

Lady Grey

Be pitiful, dread lord, and grant it then.

King Edward IV

Lords, give us leave, I'll try this widow's wit.

Gloucester

(From Aside to Clarence) Ay, good leave have you

For you will have leave, till youth take leave and leave you to the crutch.

(Gloucester and Clarence retire)

King Edward IV

Now tell me, madam, do you love your children?

Lady Grey

Ay, full as dearly as I love myself.

King Edward IV

And would you not do much to do them good?

Lady Grey

To do them good, I would sustain some harm.

King Edward IV

Then get your husband's lands, to do them good.

Lady Grey

Therefore I came unto your majesty.

King Edward IV

I'll tell you how these lands are to be got.

Lady Grey

So shall you bind me to your highness' service.

King Edward IV

What service wilt thou do me, if I give them?

Lady Grey

What you command, that rests in me to do.

King Edward IV

But you will take exceptions to my boon.

Lady Grey

No, gracious lord, except I cannot do it.

King Edward IV

Ay, but thou canst do what I mean to ask.

Lady Grey

Why, then I will do what your grace commands.

Gloucester

(**From Aside to Clarence**) He plies her hard; and much rain wears the marble.

Clarence

(**From Aside to Gloucester**) As red as fire! nay, then her wax must melt.

Lady Grey

Why stops my lord, shall I not hear my task?

King Edward IV

An easy task

It is but to love a king.

Lady Grey

That's soon performed, because I am a subject.

King Edward IV

Why, then, thy husband's lands I freely give thee.

Lady Grey

I take my leave with many thousand thanks.

Gloucester

(From Aside to Clarence) The match is made; she seals it with a curtsy.

King Edward IV

But stay thee, it is the fruits of love I mean.

Lady Grey

The fruits of love I mean, my loving liege.

King Edward IV

Ay, but, I fear me, in another sense.

What love, think'st thou, I sue so much to get?

Lady Grey

My love till death, my humble thanks, my prayers

That love which virtue begs and virtue grants.

King Edward IV

No, by my troth, I did not mean such love.

Lady Grey

Why, then you mean not as I thought you did.

King Edward IV

But now you partly may perceive my mind.

Lady Grey

My mind will never grant what I perceive your highness aims at, if I aim aright.

King Edward IV

To tell thee plain, I aim to lie with thee.

Lady Grey

To tell you plain, I had rather lie in prison.

King Edward IV

Why, then thou shalt not have thy husband's lands.

Lady Grey

Why, then mine honesty shall be my dower

For by that loss I will not purchase them.

King Edward IV

Therein thou wrong'st thy children mightily.

Lady Grey

Herein your highness wrongs both them and me.

But, mighty lord, this merry inclination accords not with the sadness of my suit, please you dismiss me either with 'ay' or 'no.'

King Edward IV

Ay, if thou wilt say 'ay' to my request

No if thou dost say 'no' to my demand.

Lady Grey

Then, no, my lord.

My suit is at an end.

Gloucester

(From Aside to Clarence) The widow likes him not, she knits her brows.

Clarence

(From Aside to Gloucester) He is the bluntest wooer in Christendom.

King Edward IV

(From Aside) Her looks do argue her replete with modesty

Her words do show her wit incomparable

All her perfections challenge sovereignty, one way or other, she is for a king

She shall be my love, or else my queen…

Say that King Edward take thee for his queen?

Lady Grey

It is better said than done, my gracious lord, I am a subject fit to jest withal, but far unfit to be a sovereign.

King Edward IV

Sweet widow, by my state I swear to thee, I speak no more than what my soul intends

That is, to enjoy thee for my love.

Lady Grey

And that is more than I will yield unto, I know I am too mean to be your queen and yet too good to be your concubine.

King Edward IV

You cavil, widow, I did mean, my queen.

Lady Grey

It will grieve your grace my sons should call you father.

King Edward IV

No more than when my daughters call thee mother.

Thou art a widow, and thou hast some children

By God's mother, I, being but a bachelor have other some, why it is a happy thing to be the father unto many sons.

Answer no more, for thou shalt be my queen.

Gloucester

(From Aside to Clarence) The ghostly father now hath done his shrift.

Clarence

(From Aside to Gloucester) When he was made a shriver, it was for shift.

King Edward IV

Brothers, you muse what chat we two have had.

Gloucester

The widow likes it not, for she looks very sad.

King Edward IV

You'll think it strange if I should marry her.

Clarence

To whom, my lord?

King Edward IV

Why, Clarence, to myself.

Gloucester

That would be ten days' wonder at the least.

Clarence

That's a day longer than a wonder lasts.

Gloucester

By so much is the wonder in extremes.

King Edward IV

Well, jest on, brothers, I can tell you both her suit is granted for her husband's lands.

(A Nobleman enters)

Nobleman

My gracious lord, Henry your foe is taken and brought your prisoner to your palace gate.

King Edward IV

See that he be conveyed unto the Tower, and go we brothers, to the man that took him, to question of his apprehension.

Widow, go you along. Lords, use her honourably.

(All exit but Gloucester)

Gloucester

Ay, Edward will use women honourably.

Would he were wasted, marrow, bones and all, that from his loins no hopeful branch may spring, to cross me from the golden time I look for!

And yet, between my soul's desire and me…

The lustful Edward's title buried…

Is Clarence, Henry, and his son young Edward, and all the unlooked for issue of their bodies to take their rooms were I can place myself a cold premeditation for my purpose!

Why, then, I do but dream on sovereignty

Like one that stands upon a promontory and spies a far-off shore where he would tread, wishing his foot were equal with his eye, and chides the sea that sunders him from thence saying, he'll lade it dry to have his way

So do I wish the crown, being so far off

So I chide the means that keeps me from it

So I say, I'll cut the causes off, flattering me with impossibilities.

My eye's too quick, my heart overweens too much unless my hand and strength could equal them.

Well, say there is no kingdom then for Richard

What other pleasure can the world afford?

I'll make my heaven in a lady's lap and deck my body in gay ornaments, and witch sweet ladies with my words and looks.

Oh miserable thought! and more unlikely than to accomplish twenty golden crowns!

Why, love forswore me in my mother's womb, and for I should not deal in her soft laws

She did corrupt frail nature with some bribe to shrink mine arm up like a withered shrub

To make an envious mountain on my back, where sits deformity to mock my body

To shape my legs of an unequal size

To disproportion me in every part like to a chaos or an unlicked bear-whelp that carries no impression like the dam.

And am I then a man to be beloved?

Oh monstrous fault, to harbour such a thought!

Then, since this earth affords no joy to me, but to command, to cheque, to overbear such as are of better person than myself

I'll make my heaven to dream upon the crown, and whiles I live to account this world

Hell until my mis-shaped trunk that bears this head ne round impaled with a glorious crown.

And yet I know not how to get the crown, for many lives stand between me and home, like one lost in a thorny wood that rends the thorns, and is rent with the thorns seeking a way and straying from the way

Not knowing how to find the open air, but toiling desperately to find it out...

Torment myself to catch the English crown, and from that torment I will free myself, or hew my way out with a bloody axe.

Why, I can smile, and murder whiles I smile, and cry content to that which grieves my heart and wet my cheeks with artificial tears, and frame my face to all occasions.

I'll drown more sailors than the mermaid shall

I'll slay more gazers than the basilisk, I'll play the orator as well as Nestor, deceive more slily than Ulysses could, and like a Sinon, take another Troy.

I can add colours to the chameleon, change shapes with Proteus for advantages and set the murderous Machiavel to school.

Can I do this, and cannot get a crown?

Tut, were it farther off, I'll pluck it down. **(Exit)**

Act 3 Scene 3

France. King Lewis XI's palace.

(Flourish)

(King Lewis XI, his sister Bona, his Admiral, called Bourbon, Prince Edward, Queen Margaret, and Oxford enter)

(King Lewis XI sits, and riseth up again)

King Lewis XI

Fair Queen of England, worthy Margaret, sit down with us, it ill befits thy state and birth, that thou shouldst stand while Lewis doth sit.

Queen Margaret

No, mighty King of France: now Margaret must strike her sail and learn awhile to serve where kings command.

I was, I must confess, great Albion's queen in former golden days, but now mischance hath trod my title down and with dishonour laid me on the ground

Where I must take like seat unto my fortune and to my humble seat conform myself.

King Lewis XI

Why, say, fair queen, whence springs this deep despair?

Queen Margaret

From such a cause as fills mine eyes with tears and stops my tongue, while heart is drowned in cares.

King Lewis XI

Whatever it be, be thou still like thyself and sit thee by our side, seats her by him

Yield not thy neck to fortune's yoke, but let thy dauntless mind still ride in triumph over all mischance.

Be plain, Queen Margaret, and tell thy grief

It shall be eased, if France can yield relief.

Queen Margaret

Those gracious words revive my drooping thoughts and give my tongue-tied sorrows leave to speak.

Now, therefore, be it known to noble Lewis, that Henry, sole possessor of my love is of a king become a banished man, and forced to live in Scotland a forlorn

While proud ambitious Edward Duke of York takes the regal title and the seat of England's true-anointed lawful king.

This is the cause that I, poor Margaret, with this my son, Prince Edward, Henry's heir am come to crave thy just and lawful aid

If thou fail us, all our hope is done, Scotland hath will to help, but cannot help our people and our peers are both misled

Our treasures seized, our soldiers put to flight and as thou seest, ourselves in heavy plight.

King Lewis XI

Renowned queen, with patience calm the storm while we bethink a means to break it off.

Queen Margaret

The more we stay, the stronger grows our foe.

King Lewis XI

The more I stay, the more I'll succor thee.

Queen Margaret

Oh, but impatience waiteth on true sorrow.

And see where comes the breeder of my sorrow!

(Warwick enters)

King Lewis XI

What's he approacheth boldly to our presence?

Queen Margaret

Our Earl of Warwick, Edward's greatest friend.

King Lewis XI

Welcome, brave Warwick! What brings thee to France?

(He descends, She ariseth)

Queen Margaret

Ay, now begins a second storm to rise

For this is he that moves both wind and tide.

Warwick

From worthy Edward, King of Albion, my lord and sovereign and thy vowed friend, I come in kindness and unfeigned love

First, to do greetings to thy royal person and then to crave a league of amity, and lastly to confirm that amity with a nuptial knot if thou vouchsafe to grant that virtuous Lady Bona, thy fair sister to England's king in lawful marriage.

Queen Margaret

(From Aside) If that go forward, Henry's hope is done.

Warwick

(To Bona) And gracious madam, in our king's behalf,

I am commanded with your leave and favour, Humbly to kiss your hand and with my tongue to tell the passion of my sovereign's heart

Where fame, late entering at his heedful ears hath placed thy beauty's image and thy virtue

Queen Margaret

King Lewis and Lady Bona, hear me speak, before you answer Warwick.

His demand springs not from Edward's well-meant honest love but from deceit bred by necessity

For how can tyrants safely govern home unless abroad they purchase great alliance?

To prove him tyrant this reason may suffice, that Henry liveth still, but were he dead, yet here Prince Edward stands, King Henry's son.

Look, therefore, Lewis, that by this league and marriage thou draw not on thy danger and dishonour

For though usurpers sway the rule awhile, yet heavens are just, and time suppresseth wrongs.

Warwick

Injurious Margaret!

Prince Edward

And why not queen?

Warwick

Because thy father Henry did take

Thou no more are prince than she is queen.

Oxford

Then Warwick disannuls great John of Gaunt, which did subdue the greatest part of Spain

After John of Gaunt, Henry the Fourth, whose wisdom was a mirror to the wisest

After that wise prince, Henry the Fifth, who by his prowess conquered all France, from these our Henry lineally descends.

Warwick

Oxford, how haps it, in this smooth discourse, you told not how Henry the Sixth hath lost all that which Henry Fifth had gotten?

Methinks these peers of France should smile at that.

But for the rest, you tell a pedigree of threescore and two years

A silly time to make prescription for a kingdom's worth.

Oxford

Why, Warwick, canst thou speak against thy liege, whom thou obeyed'st thirty and six years, and not bewray thy treason with a blush?

Warwick

Can Oxford, that did ever fence the right, now buckler falsehood with a pedigree?

For shame! leave Henry, and call Edward king.

Oxford

Call him my king by whose injurious doom my elder brother, the Lord Aubrey there, was done to death?

And more than so, my father, even in the downfall of his mellowed years, when nature brought him to the door of death?

No, Warwick, no; while life upholds this arm, this arm upholds the house of Lancaster.

Warwick

And I the house of York.

King Lewis XI

At our request, Queen Margaret, Prince Edward, and Oxford, Vouchsafe, are to stand aside, while I use further conference with Warwick.

(They stand aloof)

Queen Margaret

Heavens grant that Warwick's words bewitch him not!

King Lewis XI

Now Warwick, tell me, even upon thy conscience, is Edward your true king?

For I were loath to link with him that were not lawful chosen.

Warwick

Thereon I pawn my credit and mine honour.

King Lewis XI

But is he gracious in the people's eye?

Warwick

The more that Henry was unfortunate.

King Lewis XI

Then further, all dissembling set aside, tell me for truth the measure of his love unto our sister Bona.

Warwick

Such it seems as may beseem a monarch like himself.

Myself have often heard him say and swear that this his love was an eternal plant, whereof the root was fixed in virtue's ground, the leaves and fruit maintained with beauty's sun exempt from envy, but not from disdain unless the Lady Bona quit his pain.

King Lewis XI

Now, sister, let us hear your firm resolve.

Bona

Your grant, or your denial, shall be mine:

(To Warwick)

Yet I confess that often ere this day, when I have heard your king's desert recounted, mine ear hath tempted judgment to desire.

King Lewis XI

Then, Warwick, thus: our sister shall be Edward's

Now forthwith shall articles be drawn touching the jointure that your king must make, which with her dowry shall be counterpoised.

Draw near, Queen Margaret, and be a witness that Bona shall be wife to the English king.

Prince Edward

To Edward, but not to the English king.

Queen Margaret

Deceitful Warwick! it was thy device by this alliance to make void my suit, before thy coming Lewis was Henry's friend.

King Lewis XI

And still is friend to him and Margaret, but if your title to the crown be weak, as may appear by Edward's good success, then it is but reason that I be released from giving aid which late I promised.

Yet shall you have all kindness at my hand that your estate requires and mine can yield.

Warwick

Henry now lives in Scotland at his ease, where having nothing, nothing can he lose and as for you yourself, our quondam queen

You have a father able to maintain you and better it were you troubled him than France.

Queen Margaret

Peace, impudent and shameless Warwick peace, proud setter up and puller down of kings!

I will not hence, till with my talk and tears both full of truth, I make King Lewis behold thy sly conveyance and thy lord's false love

For both of you are birds of selfsame feather.

(Post blows a horn within)

King Lewis XI

Warwick, this is some post to us or thee.

(A Post enters)

Post

(To Warwick) My lord ambassador, these letters are for you, sent from your brother, Marquess Montague

(To King Lewis XI)

These from our king unto your majesty

(To Queen Margaret)

And, madam, these for you; from whom I know not.

They all read their letters

Oxford

I like it well that our fair queen and mistress smiles at her news, while Warwick frowns at his.

Prince Edward

Nay, mark how Lewis stamps, as he were nettled, I hope all's for the best.

King Lewis XI

Warwick, what are thy news? and yours, fair queen?

Queen Margaret

Mine, such as fill my heart with unhoped joys.

Warwick

Mine, full of sorrow and heart's discontent.

King Lewis XI

What! has your king married the Lady Grey!

And now, to soothe your forgery and his sends me a paper to persuade me patience?

Is this the alliance that he seeks with France?

Dare he presume to scorn us in this manner?

Queen Margaret

I told your majesty as much before, this proveth Edward's love and Warwick's honesty.

Warwick

King Lewis, I here protest, in sight of heaven and by the hope I have of heavenly bliss that I am clear from this misdeed of Edward's no more my king, for he dishonours me but most himself if he could see his shame.

Did I forget that by the house of York my father came untimely to his death?

Did I let pass the abuse done to my niece?

Did I impale him with the regal crown?

Did I put Henry from his native right?

And am I guerdon'd at the last with shame?

Shame on himself! for my desert is honour and to repair my honour lost for him, I here renounce him and return to Henry.

My noble queen, let former grudges pass and henceforth I am thy true servitor, I will revenge his wrong to Lady Bona and replant Henry in his former state.

Queen Margaret

Warwick, these words have turn'd my hate to love

I forgive and quite forget old faults and joy that thou becomest King Henry's friend.

Warwick

So much his friend, ay, his unfeigned friend, that if King Lewis vouchsafe to furnish us with some few bands of chosen soldiers, I'll undertake to land them on our coast and force the tyrant from his seat by war.

It is not his new-made bride shall succor him and as for Clarence, as my letters tell me, he's very likely now to fall from him for matching more for wanton lust than honour, or than for strength and safety of our country.

Bona

Dear brother, how shall Bona be revenged but by thy help to this distressed queen?

Queen Margaret

Renowned prince, how shall poor Henry live, unless thou rescue him from foul despair?

Bona

My quarrel and this English queen's are one.

Warwick

And mine, fair lady Bona, joins with yours.

King Lewis XI

And mine with hers, and thine, and Margaret's.

Therefore at last I firmly am resolved you shall have aid.

Queen Margaret

Let me give humble thanks for all at once.

King Lewis XI

Then, England's messenger, return in post and tell false Edward, thy supposed king that Lewis of France is sending over masquers to revel it with him and his new bride

Thou seest what's past, go fear thy king withal.

Bona

Tell him, in hope he'll prove a widower shortly, I'll wear the willow garland for his sake.

Queen Margaret

Tell him, my mourning weeds are laid aside and I am ready to put armour on.

Warwick

Tell him from me that he hath done me wrong and therefore I'll uncrown him were it be long.

There's thy reward: be gone.

(Post exits)

King Lewis XI

But, Warwick, thou and Oxford with five thousand men shall cross the seas, and bid false Edward battle

As occasion serves, this noble queen and prince shall follow with a fresh supply.

Yet, ere thou go, but answer me one doubt what pledge have we of thy firm loyalty?

Warwick

This shall assure my constant loyalty that if our queen and this young prince agree, I'll join mine eldest daughter and my joy to him forthwith in holy wedlock bands.

Queen Margaret

Yes, I agree, and thank you for your motion.

Son Edward, she is fair and virtuous, therefore delay not, give thy hand to Warwick

With thy hand, thy faith irrevocable, that only Warwick's daughter shall be thine.

Prince Edward

Yes, I accept her, for she well deserves it

Here, to pledge my vow I give my hand.

(He gives his hand to Warwick)

King Lewis XI

Why stay we now?

These soldiers shall be levied and thou, Lord Bourbon, our high admiral, shalt waft them over with our royal fleet.

I long till Edward fall by war's mischance, for mocking marriage with a dame of France.

(All exit but Warwick)

Warwick

I came from Edward as ambassador, but I return his sworn and mortal foe

The matter of marriage was the charge he gave me, but dreadful war shall answer his demand.

Had he none else to make a stale but me?

Then none but I shall turn his jest to sorrow.

I was the chief that raised him to the crown and I'll be chief to bring him down again, not that I pity Henry's misery, but seek revenge on Edward's mockery. **(Exit)**

Act 4 Scene 1

London. The palace.

(**Gloucester**, **Clarence**, **Somerset**, and **Montague** enters)

Gloucester

Now tell me, brother Clarence, what think you of this new marriage with the Lady Grey?

Hath not our brother made a worthy choice?

Clarence

Alas, you know, 'tis far from hence to France

How could he stay till Warwick made return?

Somerset

My lords, forbear this talk; here comes the king.

Gloucester

And his well-chosen bride.

Clarence

I mind to tell him plainly what I think.

(Flourish)

(King Edward IV attended, Queen Elizabeth, Pembroke, Stafford, Hastings, and others enter)

King Edward IV

Now, brother of Clarence, how like you our choice that you stand pensive as half malcontent?

Clarence

As well as Lewis of France, or the Earl of Warwick, which are so weak of courage and in judgment that they'll take no offence at our abuse.

King Edward IV

Suppose they take offence without a cause, they are but Lewis and Warwick, I am Edward, your king and Warwick's and must have my will.

Gloucester

And shall have your will, because our king, yet hasty marriage seldom proveth well

King Edward IV

Yea, brother Richard, are you offended too?

Gloucester

Not I

No, God forbid that I should wish them severed whom God hath joined together

Ay, and it were pity to sunder them that yoke so well together.

King Edward IV

Setting your scorns and your mislike aside, tell me some reason why the Lady Grey should not become my wife and England's queen.

And you too, Somerset and Montague, speak freely what you think.

Clarence

Then this is mine opinion: that King Lewis becomes your enemy, for mocking him about the marriage of the Lady Bona.

Gloucester

And Warwick, doing what you gave in charge, s now dishonoured by this new marriage.

King Edward IV

What if both Lewis and Warwick be appeased by such invention as I can devise?

Montague

Yet, to have joined with France in such alliance would more have strengthened this our commonwealth against foreign storms than any home-bred marriage.

Hastings

Why, knows not Montague that of itself England is safe, if true within itself?

Montague

But the safer when it is backed with France.

Hastings

It is better using France than trusting France, let us be backed with God and with the seas which He hath given for fence impregnable, and with their helps only defend ourselves

In them and in ourselves our safety lies.

Clarence

For this one speech Lord Hastings well deserves to have the heir of the Lord Hungerford.

King Edward IV

Ay, what of that? it was my will and grant

For this once my will shall stand for law.

Gloucester

And yet methinks your grace hath not done well, to give the heir and daughter of Lord Scales unto the brother of your loving bride

She better would have fitted me or Clarence, but in your bride you bury brotherhood.

Clarence

Or else you would not have bestowed the heir of the Lord Bonville on your new wife's son, and leave your brothers to go speed elsewhere.

King Edward IV

Alas, poor Clarence! is it for a wife that thou art malcontent? I will provide thee.

Clarence

In choosing for yourself, you showed your judgment, which being shallow, you give me leave to play the broker in mine own behalf

And to that end I shortly mind to leave you.

King Edward IV

Leave me, or tarry, Edward will be king and not be tied unto his brother's will.

Queen Elizabeth

My lords, before it pleased his majesty to raise my state to title of a queen, do me but right and you must all confess that I was not ignoble of descent

And meaner than myself have had like fortune.

But as this title honours me and mine, so your dislike, to whom I would be pleasing, doth cloud my joys with danger and with sorrow.

King Edward IV

My love, forbear to fawn upon their frowns, what danger or what sorrow can befall thee, so long as Edward is thy constant friend and their true sovereign, whom they must obey?

Nay, whom they shall obey, and love thee too, unless they seek for hatred at my hands

Which if they do, yet will I keep thee safe and they shall feel the vengeance of my wrath.

Gloucester

(From Aside) I hear, yet say not much, but think the more.

(A Post enters)

King Edward IV

Now, messenger, what letters or what news From France?

(Post)

My sovereign liege, no letters; and few words, but such as I, without your special pardon, dare not relate.

King Edward IV

Go to, we pardon thee therefore in brief, tell me their words as near as thou canst guess them.

What answer makes King Lewis unto our letters?

Post

At my depart, these were his very words, go tell false Edward thy supposed king, that Lewis of France is sending over masquers to revel it with him and his new bride.

King Edward IV

Is Lewis so brave? belike he thinks me Henry.

But what said Lady Bona to my marriage?

Post

These were her words, uttered with mad disdain, tell him, in hope he'll prove a widower shortly, I'll wear the willow garland for his sake.

King Edward IV

I blame not her, she could say little less

She had the wrong. But what said Henry's queen?

For I have heard that she was there in place.

Post

Tell him, quoth she, my mourning weeds are done and I am ready to put armour on.

King Edward IV

Belike she minds to play the Amazon.

But what said Warwick to these injuries?

Post

He, more incensed against your majesty than all the rest, discharged me with these words, tell him from me that he hath done me wrong and therefore I'll uncrown him were it be long.

King Edward IV

Ha! durst the traitor breathe out so proud words?

Well I will arm me, being thus forewarned, they shall have wars and pay for their presumption.

But say, is Warwick friends with Margaret?

Post

Ay, gracious sovereign; they are so linked in friendship

That young Prince Edward marries Warwick's daughter.

Clarence

Belike the elder; Clarence will have the younger.

Now, brother king, farewell, and sit you fast, for I will hence to Warwick's other daughter

That, though I want a kingdom, yet in marriage I may not prove inferior to yourself.

You that love me and Warwick, follow me.

(Clarence exits and Somerset follows)

Gloucester

(**From Aside**) Not I, my thoughts aim at a further matter I stay not for the love of Edward, but the crown.

King Edward IV

Clarence and Somerset both gone to Warwick!

Yet am I armed against the worst can happen

Haste is needful in this desperate case.

Pembroke and Stafford, you in our behalf go levy men, and make prepare for war

They are already, or quickly will be landed, myself in person will straight follow you.

(Pembroke and Stafford exit)

But, here I go, Hastings and Montague resolve my doubt.

You twain, of all the rest, are near to Warwick by blood and by alliance, tell me if you love Warwick more than me?

If it be so, then both depart to him

I rather wish you foes than hollow friends, but if you mind to hold your true obedience, give me assurance with some friendly vow that I may never have you in suspect.

Montague

So God help Montague as he proves true!

Hastings

And Hastings as he favours Edward's cause!

King Edward IV

Now, brother Richard, will you stand by us?

Gloucester

Ay, in despite of all that shall withstand you.

King Edward IV

Why, so! then am I sure of victory.

Now therefore let us hence; and lose no hour till we meet Warwick with his foreign power.

(Exit)

Act 4 Scene 2

A plain in Warwickshire.

(Warwick and Oxford enter with French soldiers)

Warwick

Trust me, my lord, all hitherto goes well

The common people by numbers swarm to us.

(Clarence and Somerset enter)

But see where Somerset and Clarence come!

Speak suddenly, my lords, are we all friends?

Clarence

Fear not that, my lord.

Warwick

Then, gentle Clarence, welcome unto Warwick

Welcome, Somerset, I hold it cowardice to rest mistrustful where a noble heart hath pawned an open hand in sign of love

Else might I think that Clarence, Edward's brother, were but a feigned friend to our proceedings, but welcome, sweet Clarence; my daughter shall be thine.

And now what rests but, in night's coverture, thy brother being carelessly encamped, his soldiers lurking in the towns about attended by a simple guard, we may surprise and take him at our pleasure?

Our scouts have found the adventure very easy, that as Ulysses and stout Diomede with sleight and manhood stole to Rhesus' tents and brought from thence the Thracian fatal steeds so we, well covered with the night's black mantle, at unawares may beat down Edward's guard and seize himself

I say not, slaughter him, for I intend but only to surprise him.

You that will follow me to this attempt, applaud the name of Henry with your leader.

They all cry, Henry!

Why, then, let's on our way in silent sort, for Warwick and his friends, God and Saint George!

(Exit)

Act 4 Scene 3

Edward's camp, near Warwick.

(Three Watchmen enter to guard King Edward IV's tent)

First Watchman

Come on, my masters, each man take his stand, the king by this is set him down to sleep.

Second Watchman

What, will he not to bed?

First Watchman

Why, no

He hath made a solemn vow never to lie and take his natural rest till Warwick or himself be quite suppressed.

Second Watchman

To-morrow then belike shall be the day if Warwick be so near as men report.

Third Watchman

But say, I pray, what nobleman is that that with the king here resteth in his tent?

First Watchman

It is the Lord Hastings, the king's chiefest friend.

Third Watchman

Oh is it so? But why commands the king that his chief followers lodge in towns about him, while he himself keeps in the cold field?

Second Watchman

It is the more honour, because more dangerous.

Third Watchman

Ay, but give me worship and quietness

I like it better than a dangerous honour.

If Warwick knew in what estate he stands,

It is to be doubted he would waken him.

First Watchman

Unless our halberds did shut up his passage.

Second Watchman

Ay, wherefore else guard we his royal tent, but to defend his person from night-foes?

(Warwick, Clarence, Oxford, Somerset, and French soldiers, enters, all silent)

Warwick

This is his tent; and see where stand his guard.

Courage, my masters! honour now or never!

But follow me, and Edward shall be ours.

First Watchman

Who goes there?

Second Watchman

Stay, or thou diest!

(Warwick and the rest cry all: Warwick! Warwick! and set upon the Guard, who fly, crying, Arm! arm!) (Warwick and the rest following them)

(Drum plays and trumpet sounds)

(Warwick, Somerset, and the rest, bringing King Edward IV out in his gown enter, sitting in a chair) (Richard and Hastings fly over the stage)

Somerset

What are they that fly there?

Warwick

Richard and Hastings, let them go here is The duke.

King Edward IV

The duke! Why, Warwick, when we parted, thou call'dst me king.

Warwick

Ay, but the case is altered, when you disgraced me in my embassade, then I degraded you from being king and come now to create you Duke of York.

Alas! how should you govern any kingdom,

That know not how to use ambassadors, nor how to be contented with one wife, nor how to use your brothers brotherly, nor how to study for the people's welfare, nor how to shroud yourself from enemies?

King Edward IV

Yea, brother of Clarence, are thou here too?

Nay, then I see that Edward needs must down.

Yet, Warwick, in despite of all mischance, of thee thyself and all thy complices, Edward will always bear himself as king, though fortune's malice overthrow my state, my mind exceeds the compass of her wheel.

Warwick

Then, for his mind, be Edward England's king

(Takes off his crown)

But Henry now shall wear the English crown and be true king indeed, thou but the shadow.

My Lord of Somerset, at my request, see that forthwith Duke Edward be conveyed unto my brother, Archbishop of York.

When I have fought with Pembroke and his fellows, I'll follow you and tell what answer Lewis and the Lady Bona send to him.

Now, for a while farewell, good Duke of York.

They lead him out forcibly

King Edward IV

What fates impose, that men must needs abide

It boots not to resist both wind and tide.

(Exits, guarded)

Oxford

What now remains, my lords, for us to do but march to London with our soldiers?

Warwick

Ay, that's the first thing that we have to do

To free King Henry from imprisonment and see him seated in the regal throne.

(Exits)

Act 4 Scene 4

London. The palace.

(Queen Elizabeth and Rivers enter)

Rivers

Madam, what makes you in this sudden change?

Queen Elizabeth

Why brother Rivers, are you yet to learn what late misfortune is befallen King Edward?

Rivers

What! loss of some pitched battle against Warwick?

Queen Elizabeth

No, but the loss of his own royal person.

Rivers

Then is my sovereign slain?

Queen Elizabeth

Ay, almost slain, for he is taken prisoner, either betrayed by falsehood of his guard or by his foe surprised at unawares, and as I further have to understand, what was new committed to the Bishop of York fell Warwick's brother, and by that our foe.

Rivers

These news I must confess are full of grief

Yet, gracious madam, bear it as you may, Warwick may lose, that now hath won the day.

Queen Elizabeth

Till then fair hope must hinder life's decay.

And I the rather wean me from despair for love of Edward's offspring in my womb, this is it that makes me bridle passion and bear with mildness my misfortune's cross

Ay, ay, for this I draw in many a tear and stop the rising of blood-sucking sighs, lest with my sighs or tears I blast or drown King Edward's fruit, true heir to the English crown.

Rivers

But, madam, where is Warwick then become?

Queen Elizabeth

I am informed that he comes towards London to set the crown once more on Henry's head

Guess thou the rest; King Edward's friends must down, but to prevent the tyrant's violence...

For trust not him that hath once broken faith...

I'll hence forthwith unto the sanctuary to save at least the heir of Edward's right, there shall I rest secure from force and fraud.

Come, therefore, let us fly while we may fly, if Warwick take us we are sure to die.

(Exit)

Act 4 Scene 5

A park near Middleham Castle in Yorkshire.

(Gloucester, Hastings, and Stanley enter)

Gloucester

Now, my Lord Hastings and Sir William Stanley, leave off to wonder why I drew you hither into this chiefest thicket of the park.

Thus stands the case, you know our king, my brother is prisoner to the bishop here at whose hands he hath good usage and great liberty, and often but attended with weak guard comes hunting this way to disport himself.

I have advertised him by secret means that if about this hour he make his way under the colour of his usual game, he shall here find his friends with horse and men to set him free from his captivity.

(King Edward IV and a Huntsman enter with him)

Huntsman

This way, my lord; for this way lies the game.

King Edward IV

Nay, this way, man: see where the huntsmen stand.

Now, brother of Gloucester, Lord Hastings, and the rest stand you thus close to steal the bishop's deer?

Gloucester

Brother, the time and case requireth haste, your horse stands ready at the park-corner.

King Edward IV

But whither shall we then?

Hastings

To Lynn, my lord and ship from thence to Flanders.

Gloucester

Well guessed, believe me

That was my meaning.

King Edward IV

Stanley, I will requite thy forwardness.

Gloucester

But wherefore stay we? It is no time to talk.

King Edward IV

Huntsman, what say'st thou? wilt thou go along?

Huntsman

Better do so than tarry and be hanged.

Gloucester

Come then, away

Let's have no more ado.

King Edward IV

Bishop, farewell: shield thee from Warwick's frown

Pray that I may repossess the crown.

(Exit)

Act 4 Scene 6

London. The Tower.

(Flourish)

(King Henry VI, Clarence, Warwick, Somerset, Henry of Richmond, Oxford, Montague, and Lieutenant of the Tower enter)

King Henry VI

Master lieutenant, now that God and friends Have shaken Edward from the regal seat and turned my captive state to liberty, my fear to hope, my sorrows unto joys, at our enlargement what are thy due fees?

Lieutenant

Subjects may challenge nothing of their sovereigns

If a humble prayer may prevail, I then crave pardon of your majesty.

King Henry VI

For what, lieutenant? for well using me?

Nay, be thou sure I'll well requite thy kindness, for that it made my imprisonment a pleasure

Ay, such a pleasure as incaged birds conceive when after many moody thoughts at last by notes of household harmony, they quite forget their loss of liberty.

Warwick, after God, thou set'st me free and chiefly therefore I thank God and thee

He was the author, thou the instrument.

Therefore, that I may conquer fortune's spite by living low, where fortune cannot hurt me and that the people of this blessed land may not be punished with my thwarting stars,

Warwick, although my head still wear the crown, I here resign my government to thee for thou art fortunate in all thy deeds.

Warwick

Your grace hath still been famed for virtuous

Now may seem as wise as virtuous by spying and avoiding fortune's malice for few men rightly temper with the stars, yet in this one thing let me blame your grace for choosing me when Clarence is in place.

Clarence

No, Warwick, thou art worthy of the sway to whom the heavens in thy nativity adjudged an olive branch and laurel crown, as likely to be blest in peace and war

Therefore I yield thee my free consent.

Warwick

And I choose Clarence only for protector.

King Henry VI

Warwick and Clarence give me both your hands, now join your hands, and with your hands your hearts, that no dissension hinder government

I make you both protectors of this land while I myself will lead a private life, and in devotion spend my latter days to sin's rebuke and my Creator's praise.

Warwick

What answers Clarence to his sovereign's will?

Clarence

That he consents, if Warwick yield consent

For on thy fortune I repose myself.

Warwick

Why, then, though loath, yet must I be content, we'll yoke together, like a double shadow to Henry's body and supply his place

I mean, in bearing weight of government while he enjoys the honour and his ease.

Clarence, now then it is more than needful forthwith that Edward be pronounced a traitor and all his lands and goods be confiscate.

Clarence

What else? and that succession be determined.

Warwick

Ay, therein Clarence shall not want his part.

King Henry VI

But, with the first of all your chief affairs, let me entreat, for I command no more that Margaret your queen and my son Edward be sent for, to return from France with speed

Till I see them here, by doubtful fear my joy of liberty is half eclipsed.

Clarence

It shall be done, my sovereign, with all speed.

King Henry VI

My Lord of Somerset, what youth is that, of whom you seem to have so tender care?

Somerset

My liege, it is young Henry, earl of Richmond.

King Henry VI

Come hither, England's hope.

Lays his hand on his head if secret powers suggest but truth to my divining thoughts, this pretty lad will prove our country's bliss.

His looks are full of peaceful majesty, his head by nature framed to wear a crown, his hand to wield a sceptre and himself likely in time to bless a regal throne.

Make much of him, my lords, for this is he must help you more than you are hurt by me.

(A Post enter)

Warwick

What news, my friend?

Post

That Edward is escaped from your brother, and fled as he hears since, to Burgundy.

Warwick

Unsavoury news! but how made he escape?

Post

He was conveyed by Richard Duke of Gloucester and the Lord Hastings, who attended him in secret ambush on the forest side and from the bishop's huntsmen rescued him

For hunting was his daily exercise.

Warwick

My brother was too careless of his charge.

But let us hence, my sovereign, to provide a salve for any sore that may betide.

(All but Somerset, Henry of Richmond, and Oxford exit)

Somerset

My lord, I like not of this flight of Edward's

Doubtless Burgundy will yield him help and we shall have more wars before 't be long.

As Henry's late presaging prophecy did glad my heart with hope of this young Richmond, so doth my heart misgive me in these conflicts

What may befall him, to his harm and ours, therefore, Lord Oxford to prevent the worst forthwith we'll send him hence to Brittany, till storms be past of civil enmity.

Oxford

Ay, for if Edward repossess the crown, it is like that Richmond with the rest shall down.

Somerset

It shall be so; he shall to Brittany.

Come, therefore, let's about it speedily.

(Exit)

Act 4 Scene 7

Before York.

(Flourish)

(King Edward IV, Gloucester, Hastings, and Soldiers enter)

King Edward IV

Now, brother Richard, Lord Hastings and the rest, yet thus far fortune maketh us amends and says that once more I shall interchange my waned state for Henry's regal crown.

Well have we passed and now repass'd the seas and brought desired help from Burgundy, what then remains, we being thus arrived from Ravenspurgh haven before the gates of York, but that we enter, as into our dukedom?

Gloucester

The gates made fast! Brother, I like not this

Many men that stumble at the threshold are well foretold that danger lurks within.

King Edward IV

Tush, man, abodements must not now affright us, by fair or foul means we must enter in, for hither will our friends repair to us.

Hastings

My liege, I'll knock once more to summon them.

(On the walls, the Mayor of York and his Brethren enter)

Mayor

My lords, we were forewarned of your coming and shut the gates for safety of ourselves

For now we owe allegiance unto Henry.

King Edward IV

But, master mayor, if Henry be your king, yet Edward at the least is Duke of York.

Mayor

True, my good lord; I know you for no less.

King Edward IV

Why, and I challenge nothing but my dukedom, as being well content with that alone.

Gloucester

(From Aside) But when the fox hath once got in his nose, he'll soon find means to make the body follow.

Hastings

Why, master mayor, why stand you in a doubt?

Open the gates; we are King Henry's friends.

Mayor

Ay, say you so? the gates shall then be opened.

(They descend)

Gloucester

A wise stout captain, and soon persuaded!

Hastings

The good old man would fain that all were well, so it were not long of him

Being entered, I doubt not, not I, but we shall soon persuade both him and all his brothers unto reason.

(The Mayor and two Aldermen enter below)

King Edward IV

So, master mayor, these gates must not be shut but in the night or in the time of war.

What! fear not, man, but yield me up the keys;

(Takes his keys)

For Edward will defend the town and thee and all those friends that deign to follow me.

(March)

(Montgomery enters with drum and soldiers)

Gloucester

Brother, this is Sir John Montgomery, our trusty friend, unless I be deceived.

King Edward IV

Welcome, Sir John! But why come you in arms?

Montague

To help King Edward in his time of storm, as every loyal subject ought to do.

King Edward IV

Thanks, good Montgomery

We now forget our title to the crown and only claim our dukedom till God please to send the rest.

Montague

Then fare you well, for I will hence again, I came to serve a king and not a duke.

Drummer, strike up, and let us march away.

(The drum begins to march)

King Edward IV

Nay, stay, Sir John, a while, and we'll debate by what safe means the crown may be recovered.

Montague

What talk you of debating? in few words, if you'll not here proclaim yourself our king I'll leave you to your fortune and be gone, to keep them back that come to succor you

Why shall we fight, if you pretend no title?

Gloucester

Why, brother, wherefore stand you on nice points?

King Edward IV

When we grow stronger, then we'll make our claim, till then, it is wisdom to conceal our meaning

Hastings

Away with scrupulous wit! now arms must rule.

Gloucester

And fearless minds climb soonest unto crowns.

Brother, we will proclaim you out of hand the bruit thereof will bring you many friends.

King Edward IV

Then be it as you will

It is my right and Henry but usurps the diadem.

Montague

Ay, now my sovereign speaketh like himself

Now will I be Edward's champion.

Hastings

Sound trumpet

Edward shall be here proclaimed

Come, fellow-soldier, make thou proclamation.

(Flourish)

Soldier

Edward the Fourth, by the grace of God, king of England and France, and lord of Ireland, & company.

Montague

And whosoever gainsays King Edward's right, by this I challenge him to single fight.

(Throws down his gauntlet)

All

Long live Edward the Fourth!

King Edward IV

Thanks, brave Montgomery

Thanks unto you all, if fortune serve me, I'll requite this kindness.

Now, for this night, let's harbour here in York

When the morning sun shall raise his car above the border of this horizon, we'll forward towards Warwick and his mates

For well I wot that Henry is no soldier.

Ah, froward Clarence! how evil it beseems thee to flatter Henry and forsake thy brother!

Yet, as we may, we'll meet both thee and Warwick.

Come on, brave soldiers: doubt not of the day, and that once gotten, doubt not of large pay.

(Exit)

Act 4 Scene 8

London. The palace.

(Flourish)

(King Henry VI, Warwick, Montague, Clarence, Exeter, and Oxford enter)

Warwick

What counsel, lords? Edward from Belgia, with hasty Germans and blunt Hollanders, hath passed in safety through the narrow seas and with his troops doth march amain to London

Many giddy people flock to him.

King Henry VI

Let's levy men, and beat him back again.

Clarence

A little fire is quickly trodden out

Which being suffered, rivers cannot quench.

Warwick

In Warwickshire I have true-hearted friends not mutinous in peace yet bold in war

Those will I muster up, and thou son Clarence, shalt stir up in Suffolk, Norfolk, and in Kent the knights and gentlemen to come with thee

Thou, brother Montague, in Buckingham, Northampton and in Leicestershire shalt find men well inclined to hear what thou command'st

Thou, brave Oxford, wondrous well beloved in Oxfordshire shalt muster up thy friends.

My sovereign, with the loving citizens, like to his island girt in with the ocean or modest Dian circled with her nymphs, shall rest in London till we come to him.

Fair lords, take leave and stand not to reply.

Farewell, my sovereign.

King Henry VI

Farewell, my Hector, and my Troy's true hope.

Clarence

In sign of truth, I kiss your highness' hand.

King Henry VI

Well-minded Clarence, be thou fortunate!

Montague

Comfort, my lord; and so I take my leave.

Oxford

And thus I seal my truth, and bid adieu.

King Henry VI

Sweet Oxford, and my loving Montague and all at once, once more a happy farewell

Warwick

Farewell, sweet lords: let's meet at Coventry.

(All but King Henry VI and Exeter exit)

King Henry VI

Here at the palace I will rest awhile.

Cousin of Exeter, what thinks your lordship?

Methinks the power that Edward hath in field should not be able to encounter mine.

Exeter

The doubt is that he will seduce the rest.

King Henry VI

That's not my fear

My meed hath got me fame, I have not stopped mine ears to their demands, nor posted off their suits with slow delays

My pity hath been balm to heal their wounds, my mildness hath allayed their swelling griefs

My mercy dried their water-flowing tears, I have not been desirous of their wealth, nor much oppressed them with great subsidies.

Nor forward of revenge, though they much erred, then why should they love Edward more than me?

No, Exeter, these graces challenge grace, and when the lion fawns upon the lamb, the lamb will never cease to follow him.

(Shout within: A Lancaster! A Lancaster!)

Exeter

Hark, hark, my lord! what shouts are these?

(King Edward IV, Gloucester, and soldiers enter)

King Edward IV

Seize on the shame-faced Henry, bear him hence

Once again proclaim us King of England.

You are the fount that makes small brooks to flow, now stops thy spring

My sea shall suck them dry and swell so much the higher by their web.

Hence with him to the Tower

Let him not speak.

(Some exit with King Henry VI)

And, lords, towards Coventry bend we our course where peremptory Warwick now remains

The sun shines hot

If we use delay, cold biting winter mars our hoped-for hay.

Gloucester

Away betimes, before his forces join and take the great-grown traitor unawares, brave warriors, march amain towards Coventry.

(Exit)

Act 5 Scene 1

Coventry.

(Warwick, the Mayor of Coventry, two Messengers, and others enter upon the walls)

Warwick

Where is the post that came from valiant Oxford?

How far hence is thy lord, mine honest fellow?

First Messenger

By this at Dunsmore, marching hitherward.

Warwick

How far off is our brother Montague?

Where is the post that came from Montague?

Second Messenger

By this at Daintry, with a puissant troop.

(Sir John Somerville enters)

Warwick

Say, Somerville, what says my loving son?

And, by thy guess, how nigh is Clarence now?

Somerset

At Southam I did leave him with his forces and do expect him here some two hours hence.

(Drum heard)

Warwick

Then Clarence is at hand, I hear his drum.

Somerset

It is not his, my lord; here Southam lies

The drum your honour hears marcheth from Warwick.

Warwick

Who should that be? belike, unlook'd-for friends.

Somerset

They are at hand, and you shall quickly know.

(March)

(Flourish)

King Edward IV, Gloucester, and soldiers enter)

King Edward IV

Go, trumpet, to the walls, and sound a meeting.

Gloucester

See how the surly Warwick mans the wall!

Warwick

Oh unbid spite! Is sportful Edward come?

Where slept our scouts, or how are they seduced, that we could hear no news of his repair?

King Edward IV

Now, Warwick, wilt thou open the city gates speak gentle words and humbly bend thy knee, call Edward king and at his hands beg mercy?

And he shall pardon thee these outrages.

Warwick

Nay, rather, wilt thou draw thy forces hence, confess who set thee up and plucked thee own, call Warwick patron and be penitent?

And thou shalt still remain the Duke of York.

Gloucester

I thought, at least, he would have said the king

Or did he make the jest against his will?

Warwick

Is not a dukedom, sir, a goodly gift?

Gloucester

Ay, by my faith, for a poor earl to give, I'll do thee service for so good a gift.

Warwick

It was I that gave the kingdom to thy brother.

King Edward IV

Why then 'tis mine, if but by Warwick's gift.

Warwick

Thou art no Atlas for so great a weight, and weakling, Warwick takes his gift again

Henry is my king, Warwick his subject.

King Edward IV

But Warwick's king is Edward's prisoner, and gallant Warwick do but answer this, what is the body when the head is off?

Gloucester

Alas, that Warwick had no more forecast, but whiles he thought to steal the single ten, the king was slily fingered from the deck!

You left poor Henry at the Bishop's palace, and ten to one, you'll meet him in the Tower.

Edward

It is even so; yet you are Warwick still.

Gloucester

Come, Warwick, take the time; kneel down, kneel down

Nay, when? strike now, or else the iron cools.

Warwick

I had rather chop this hand off at a blow and with the other fling it at thy face, than bear so low a sail, to strike to thee.

King Edward IV

Sail how thou canst, have wind and tide thy friend, this hand fast wound about thy coal-black hair shall, whiles thy head is warm and new cut off, write in the dust this sentence with thy blood

Wind-changing Warwick now can change no more.

(Oxford enters with drum and colours)

Warwick

O cheerful colours! see where Oxford comes!

Oxford

Oxford, Oxford, for Lancaster!

He and his forces enter the city

Gloucester

The gates are open, let us enter too.

King Edward IV

So other foes may set upon our backs.

Stand we in good array; for they no doubt will issue out again and bid us battle, if not, the city being but of small defence, we'll quickly rouse the traitors in the same.

Warwick

Oh welcome, Oxford! for we want thy help.

(Montague enters with drum and colours)

Montague

Montague, Montague, for Lancaster!

He and his forces enter the city

Gloucester

Thou and thy brother both shall buy this treason even with the dearest blood your bodies bear.

King Edward IV

The harder matched, the greater victory, my mind presageth happy gain and conquest.

(Somerset enters with drum and colours)

Somerset

Somerset, Somerset, for Lancaster!

He and his forces enter the city

Gloucester

Two of thy name, both Dukes of Somerset have sold their lives unto the house of York and thou shalt be the third if this sword hold.

(Clarence enters with drum and colours)

Warwick

And lord, where George of Clarence sweeps along of force enough to bid his brother battle

With whom an upright zeal to right prevails more than the nature of a brother's love!

Come, Clarence, come

Thou wilt, if Warwick call.

Clarence

Father of Warwick, know you what this means?

Taking his red rose out of his hat

Look here, I throw my infamy at thee, I will not ruinate my father's house who gave his blood to lime the stones together, and set up Lancaster.

Why, trow'st thou Warwick, that Clarence is so harsh, so blunt, unnatural, to bend the fatal instruments of war against his brother and his lawful king?

Perhaps thou wilt object my holy oath to keep that oath were more impiety than Jephthah's, when he sacrificed his daughter.

I am so sorry for my trespass made that, to deserve well at my brother's hands, I here proclaim myself thy mortal foe with resolution wheresoever, I meet thee…

As I will meet thee, if thou stir abroad…

To plague thee for thy foul misleading me and so, proud-hearted Warwick, I defy thee and to my brother turn my blushing cheeks.

Pardon me, Edward, I will make amends, and Richard, do not frown upon my faults for I will henceforth be no more unconstant.

King Edward IV

Now welcome more, and ten times more beloved, than if thou never hadst deserved our hate.

Gloucester

Welcome, good Clarence; this is brotherlike.

Warwick

Oh passing traitor, perjured and unjust!

King Edward IV

What, Warwick, wilt thou leave the town and fight?

Or shall we beat the stones about thine ears?

Warwick

Alas, I am not coop'd here for defence!

I will away towards Barnet presently and bid thee battle, Edward, if thou darest.

King Edward IV

Yes, Warwick, Edward dares, and leads the way.

Lords, to the field

Saint George and victory!

(King Edward and his company exit)

(March)

Warwick and his company follow

Act 5 Scene 2

A field of battle near Barnet.

(Alarum and excursions)

(King Edward IV enters bringing forth Warwick wounded)

King Edward IV

So, lie thou there: die thou, and die our fear

For Warwick was a bug that feared us all.

Now Montague, sit fast

I seek for thee, that Warwick's bones may keep thine company.

(Exit)

Warwick

Ah, who is nigh? come to me, friend or foe and tell me who is victor, York or Warwick?

Why ask I that? my mangled body shows, my blood, my want of strength, my sick heart shows.

That I must yield my body to the earth and by my fall, the conquest to my foe.

Thus yields the cedar to the axe's edge whose arms gave shelter to the princely eagle, under whose shade the ramping lion slept, whose top-branch overpeered Jupiter's spreading tree and kept low shrubs from winter's powerful wind.

These eyes, that now are dimmed with death's black veil have been as piercing as the mid-day sun, to search the secret treasons of the world

The wrinkles in my brows, now filled with blood were likened oft to kingly sepulchres

For who lived king, but I could dig his grave?

And who durst mine when Warwick bent his brow?

Lord, now my glory smeared in dust and blood!

My parks, my walks, my manors that I had.

Even now forsake me, and of all my lands is nothing left me but my body's length.

Why, what is pomp, rule, reign, but earth and dust?

And, live we how we can, yet die we must.

(Oxford and Somerset enter)

Somerset

Ah, Warwick, Warwick! wert thou as we are.

We might recover all our loss again

The queen from France hath brought a puissant power, even now we heard the news, ah, could'st thou fly!

Warwick

Why, then I would not fly.

Ah, Montague, if thou be there, sweet brother, take my hand.

And with thy lips keep in my soul awhile!

Thou lovest me not; for, brother, if thou didst, thy tears would wash this cold congealed blood that glues my lips and will not let me speak.

Come quickly, Montague, or I am dead.

Somerset

Ah, Warwick! Montague hath breathed his last

To the latest gasp cried out for Warwick and said commend me to my valiant brother.

And more he would have said, and more he spoke, which sounded like a clamour in a vault, that mought not be distinguished

At last I well might hear, delivered with a groan, oh farewell, Warwick!

Warwick

Sweet rest his soul! Fly, lords, and save yourselves for Warwick bids you all farewell to meet in heaven.

(Dies)

Oxford

Away, away, to meet the queen's great power!

Here they bear away his body.

(Exit)

Act 5 Scene 3

Another part of the field.

(Flourish)

(King Edward IV enters in triumph with Gloucester, Clarence, and the rest)

King Edward IV

Thus far our fortune keeps an upward course and we are graced with wreaths of victory.

But in the midst of this bright-shining day, I spy a black, suspicious, threatening cloud that will encounter with our glorious sun, here he attain his easeful western bed

I mean, my lords, those powers that the queen hath raised in Gallia have arrived our coast and as we hear, march on to fight with us.

Clarence

A little gale will soon disperse that cloud and blow it to the source from whence it came, the very beams will dry those vapours up, for every cloud engenders not a storm.

Gloucester

The queen is valued thirty thousand strong, and Somerset, with Oxford fled to her, if she have time to breathe be well assured her faction will be full as strong as ours.

King Edward IV

We are advertised by our loving friends that they do hold their course toward Tewksbury

We, having now the best at Barnet field, will thither straight for willingness rids way

As we march, our strength will be augmented in every county as we go along.

Strike up the drum

Cry Courage! and away.

(Exit)

Act 5 Scene 4

Plains near Tewksbury.

(March)

(Queen Margaret, Prince Edward, Somerset, Oxford, and soldiers enter)

Queen Margaret

Great lords, wise men never sit and wail their loss, but cheerly seek how to redress their harms.

What though the mast be now blown overboard, the cable broke, the holding-anchor lost and half our sailors swallowed in the flood?

Yet lives our pilot still. Is't meet that he should leave the helm and like a fearful lad with tearful eyes add water to the sea and give more strength to that which hath too much, whiles in his moan, the ship splits on the rock which industry and courage might have saved?

Ah, what a shame! ah, what a fault were this!

Say Warwick was our anchor; what of that?

And Montague our topmost; what of him?

Our slaughtered friends the tackles; what of these?

Why, is not Oxford here another anchor?

And Somerset another goodly mast?

The friends of France our shrouds and tacklings?

And, though unskilful, why not Ned and I for once allowed the skilful pilot's charge?

We will not from the helm to sit and weep, but keep our course, though the rough wind say no from shelves and rocks that threaten us with wreck.

As good to chide the waves as speak them fair.

And what is Edward but ruthless sea?

What Clarence but a quicksand of deceit?

And Richard but a ragged fatal rock?

All these the enemies to our poor bark.

Say you can swim; alas, 'tis but a while!

Tread on the sand; why, there you quickly sink, bestride the rock; the tide will wash you off, or else you famish

That's a threefold death.

This speak I, lords, to let you understand if case some one of you would fly from us, that there's no hoped-for mercy with the brothers more than with ruthless waves, with sands and rocks.

Why, courage then! What cannot be avoided it were childish weakness to lament or fear.

Prince Edward

Methinks a woman of this valiant spirit should, if a coward heard her speak these words, infuse his breast with magnanimity and make him, naked, foil a man at arms.

I speak not this as doubting any here, for did I but suspect a fearful man he should have leave to go away betimes, lest in our need he might infect another and make him of like spirit to himself.

If any such be here…

As God forbid!...

Let him depart before we need his help.

Oxford

Women and children of so high a courage and warriors faint! why, it were perpetual shame o brave young prince!

Thy famous grandfather doth live again in thee: long mayst thou live to bear his image and renew his glories!

Somerset

And he that will not fight for such a hope.

Go home to bed, and like the owl by day if he arise, be mocked and wondered at.

Queen Margaret

Thanks, gentle Somerset

Sweet Oxford, thanks.

Prince Edward

And take his thanks that yet hath nothing else.

(A Messenger enters)

Messenger

Prepare you, lords, for Edward is at hand.

Ready to fight

Therefore be resolute.

Oxford

I thought no less: it is his policy to haste thus fast, to find us unprovided.

Somerset

But he's deceived

We are in readiness.

Queen Margaret

This cheers my heart, to see your forwardness.

Oxford

Here pitch our battle; hence we will not budge.

(Flourish and march)

(King Edward IV, Gloucester, Clarence, and soldiers enter)

King Edward IV

Brave followers, yonder stands the thorny wood, which, by the heavens' assistance and your strength must by the roots be hewn up yet ere night.

I need not add more fuel to your fire, for well I wot ye blaze to burn them out give signal to the fight, and to it, lords!

Queen Margaret

Lords, knights, and gentlemen, what I should say my tears gainsay

Every word I speak, ye see I drink the water of mine eyes.

Therefore, no more but this, Henry, your sovereign is prisoner to the foe

His state taken, his realm a slaughter-house, his subjects slain, his statutes cancelled and his treasure spent

And yonder is the wolf that makes this spoil.

You fight in justice, then in God's name, lords, be valiant and give signal to the fight.

(Alarum)   (Retreat)   (Excursions)   (Exit)

Act 5 Scene 5

Another part of the field.

(Flourish)

(King Edward IV, Gloucester, Clarence, and soldiers enter with Queen Margaret, Oxford, and Somerset, prisoners)

King Edward IV

Now here a period of tumultuous broils.

Away with Oxford to Hames Castle straight, for Somerset, off with his guilty head.

Go, bear them hence; I will not hear them speak.

Oxford

For my part, I'll not trouble thee with words.

Somerset

Nor I, but stoop with patience to my fortune.

(Oxford and Somerset exit, guarded)

Queen Margaret

So part we sadly in this troublous world, to meet with joy in sweet Jerusalem.

King Edward IV

Is proclamation made, that who finds Edward shall have a high reward, and he his life?

Gloucester

It is: and lo, where youthful Edward comes!

(Soldiers enter with Prince Edward)

King Edward IV

Bring forth the gallant, let us hear him speak.

What! can so young a thorn begin to prick?

Edward, what satisfaction canst thou make for bearing arms, for stirring up my subjects and all the trouble thou hast turned me to?

Prince Edward

Speak like a subject, proud ambitious York!

Suppose that I am now my father's mouth

Resign thy chair, and where I stand kneel thou, whilst I propose the selfsame words to thee, which traitor, thou wouldst have me answer to.

Queen Margaret

Ah, that thy father had been so resolved!

Gloucester

That you might still have worn the petticoat, and never have stollen the breech from Lancaster.

Prince Edward

Let Aesop fable in a winter's night

His currish riddles sort not with this place.

Gloucester

By heaven, brat, I'll plague ye for that word.

Queen Margaret

Ay, thou wast born to be a plague to men.

Gloucester

For God's sake, take away this captive scold.

Prince Edward

Nay, take away this scolding crookback rather.

King Edward IV

Peace, wilful boy, or I will charm your tongue.

Clarence

Untutored lad, thou art too malapert.

Prince Edward

I know my duty

You are all undutiful, Lascivious Edward, and thou perjured George and thou mis-shapen **Dick**

I tell, ye all I am your better, traitors as ye are, and thou force my father's right and mine.

King Edward IV

Take that, thou likeness of this railer here.

(Stabs him)

Gloucester

Sprawl'st thou? take that, to end thy agony.

(Stabs him)

Clarence

And there's for twitting me with perjury.

(Stabs him)

Queen Margaret

Oh kill me too!

Gloucester

Marry, and shall.

Offers to kill her

King Edward IV

Hold, Richard, hold; for we have done too much.

Gloucester

Why should she live, to fill the world with words?

King Edward IV

What, doth she swoon? Use means for her recovery.

Gloucester

Clarence, excuse me to the king my brother

I'll hence to London on a serious matter, were ye come there, be sure to hear some news.

Clarence

What? what?

Gloucester

The Tower, the Tower.

(Exits)

Queen Margaret

Oh Ned, sweet Ned! speak to thy mother, boy!

Canst thou not speak? Oh traitors! murderers!

They that stabbed Caesar shed no blood at all did not offend, nor were not worthy blame if this foul deed were by to equal it

He was a man, this in respect was a child, and men never spend their fury on a child.

What's worse than murderer, that I may name it?

No, no, my heart will burst, and if I speak and I will speak, that so my heart may burst.

Butchers and villains! bloody cannibals!

How sweet a plant have you untimely cropped!

You have no children, butchers! if you had the thought of them would have stirred up remorse, but if you ever chance to have a child, look in his youth to have him so cut off as deathmen

You have rid this sweet young prince!

King Edward IV

Away with her; go, bear her hence perforce.

Queen Margaret

Nay, never bear me hence, dispatch me here, here sheathe thy sword I'll pardon thee my death, what wilt thou not?

Then, Clarence, do it thou.

Clarence

By heaven, I will not do thee so much ease.

Queen Margaret

Good Clarence, do

Sweet Clarence, do thou do it.

Clarence

Didst thou not hear me swear I would not do it?

Queen Margaret

Ay, but thou usest to forswear thyself, it was sin before, but now it is charity.

What wilt thou not? Where is that devil's butcher hard-favoured Richard?

Richard, where art thou?

Thou art not here: murder is thy alms-deed

Petitioners for blood thou nener put'st back.

King Edward IV

Away, I say

I charge ye, bear her hence.

Queen Margaret

So come to you and yours, as to this Prince!

(Exits, led out forcibly)

King Edward IV

Where's Richard gone?

Clarence

To London, all in post

As I guess, to make a bloody supper in the Tower.

King Edward IV

He's sudden, if a thing comes in his head.

Now march we hence, discharge the common sort with pay and thanks

Let's away to London and see our gentle queen how well she fares, by this I hope she hath a son for me.

(Exit)

Act 5 Scene 6

London. The Tower.

(King Henry VI and Gloucester enter with the Lieutenant, on the walls)

Gloucester

Good day, my lord. What, at your book so hard?

King Henry VI

Ay, my good lord...

My lord, I should say rather

It is sin to flatter

Good was little better, good Gloucester and good devil were alike, and both preposterous

Therefore, not good lord.

Gloucester

Sirrah, leave us to ourselves: we must confer.

(Lieutenant exits)

King Henry VI

So flies the reckless shepherd from the wolf

So first the harmless sheep doth yield his fleece and next his throat unto the butcher's knife

What scene of death hath Roscius now to act?

Gloucester

Suspicion always haunts the guilty mind

The thief doth fear each bush an officer.

King Henry VI

The bird that hath been limed in a bush with trembling wings misdoubteth every bush

And I, the hapless male to one sweet bird, have now the fatal object in my eye where my poor young was limed, was caught and killed.

Gloucester

Why, what a peevish fool was that of Crete, that taught his son the office of a fowl!

And yet, for all his wings, the fool was drowned.

King Henry VI

I, Daedalus; my poor boy, Icarus

Thy father, Minos, that denied our course

The sun that seared the wings of my sweet boy thy brother Edward, and thyself the sea whose envious gulf did swallow up his life.

Ah, kill me with thy weapon, not with words!

My breast can better brook thy dagger's point than can my ears that tragic history.

But wherefore dost thou come? Is't for my life?

Gloucester

Think'st thou I am an executioner?

King Henry VI

A persecutor, I am sure thou art, if murdering innocents be executing, why then thou art an executioner.

Gloucester

Thy son I killed for his presumption.

King Henry VI

Hadst thou been killed when first thou didst presume, Thou hadst not lived to kill a son of mine.

And thus I prophesy, that many a thousand which now mistrust no parcel of my fear and many an old man's sigh and many a widow's, and many an orphan's water-standing eye…

Men for their sons, wives for their husbands, and orphans for their parents timeless death…

Shall rue the hour that ever thou wast born.

The owl shrieked at thy birth…

An evil sign

The night-crow cried, aboding luckless time

Dogs howled, and hideous tempest shook down trees

The raven rooked her on the chimney's top and chattering pies in dismal discords sung.

Thy mother felt more than a mother's pain, and yet brought forth less than a mother's hope to wit, an indigested and deformed lump lot like the fruit of such a goodly tree.

Teeth hadst thou in thy head when thou wast born to signify thou camest to bite the world, and if the rest be true which I have heard thou camest...

Gloucester

I'll hear no more: die, prophet in thy speech

(Stabs him)

For this amongst the rest, was I ordained.

King Henry VI

Ay, and for much more slaughter after this.

God forgive my sins, and pardon thee!

(Dies)

Gloucester

What, will the aspiring blood of Lancaster sink in the ground? I thought it would have mounted.

See how my sword weeps for the poor king's death!

Oh may such purple tears be alway shed from those that wish the downfall of our house!

If any spark of life be yet remaining, down, down to hell

And say I sent thee thither

(Stabs him again)

I, that have neither pity, love, nor fear.

Indeed, it is true that Henry told me of

For I have often heard my mother say I came into the world with my legs forward, had I not reason, think ye, to make haste and seek their ruin that force our right?

The midwife wondered and the women cried oh Jesus bless us, he is born with teeth!

And so I was

Which plainly signified that I should snarl and bite and play the dog

Then, since the heavens have shaped my body so, let hell make crooked my mind to answer it.

I have no brother, I am like no brother

This word love, which graybeards call divine, be resident in men like one another and not in me, I am myself alone.

Clarence, beware

Thou keep'st me from the light, but I will sort a pitchy day for thee;

For I will buz abroad such prophecies that Edward shall be fearful of his life, and then to purge his fear, I'll be thy death.

King Henry and the prince his son are gone, Clarence thy turn is next and then the rest counting myself, but bad till I be best.

I'll throw thy body in another room and triumph, Henry, in thy day of doom.

(Exits with the body)

Act 5 Scene 7

London. The palace

(Flourish)

(King Edward IV, Queen Elizabeth, Clarence, Gloucester, Hastings, a Nurse with the young Prince, and Attendants enter)

King Edward IV

Once more we sit in England's royal throne re-purchased with the blood of enemies.

What valiant foemen, like to autumn's corn have we mowed down, in tops of all their pride!

Three Dukes of Somerset, threefold renowned for hardy and undoubted champions

Two Cliffords, as the father and the son, and two Northumberlands

Two braver men never spurred their coursers at the trumpet's sound with them, the two brave bears Warwick and Montague, that in their chains fettered the kingly lion and made the forest tremble when they roared.

Thus have we swept suspicion from our seat and made our footstool of security.

Come hither, bless and let me kiss my boy.

Young Ned, for thee thine uncles and myself have in our armours watched the winter's night went all afoot in summer's scalding heat that thou mightst repossess the crown in peace

Of our labours thou shalt reap the gain.

Gloucester

(From Aside) I'll blast his harvest, if your head were laid

For yet I am not looked on in the world.

This shoulder was ordain'd so thick to heave

Heave it shall some weight, or break my back:

Work thou the way...

Thou shalt execute.

King Edward IV

Clarence and Gloucester, love my lovely queen

Kiss your princely nephew, brothers both.

Clarence

The duty that I owe unto your majesty I seal upon the lips of this sweet babe.

Queen Elizabeth

Thanks, noble Clarence; worthy brother, thanks.

Gloucester

And, that I love the tree from whence thou sprang'st, witness the loving kiss I give the fruit.

(From Aside)

And cried all hail! when as he meant all harm.

King Edward IV

Now am I seated as my soul delights, having my country's peace and brothers' loves.

Clarence

What will your grace have done with Margaret?

Her father reignier to the king of France hath pawned the Sicils and Jerusalem and hither have they sent it for her ransom.

King Edward IV

Away with her, and waft her hence to France.

And now what rests but that we spend the time with stately triumphs, mirthful comic shows, such as befits the pleasure of the court?

Sound drums and trumpets!

Farewell sour annoy!

For here, I hope, begins our lasting joy.

(Exit)

The End

Description of Titles

The Comedy of Errors
Caught in a land of embittered woman and war, caught in months of strife, where a merchant's visit offers little natural relief. The fleeting moment of approving gold, inspire further bitterness, upon an approach to the marketplace, and then the women that occupy within them.

19 Characters

The Taming of the Shrew
Arrangements are made to spencer would be suiters to melt the splendors of a strong willed women. The winning is found pledged, influencing maids to seek their turns, and meanwhile terms required, an authentic spirit that they will/would wed soon.

34 Characters

Love's Labor's Lost
The house of a scholarly pursuit, returns into an expressive, either poetic or drunken as highlighting the gold-slur filled house of charms and dance like rhymes

19 Characters

A Midsummer Night's Dream
Journey into a land of fairies, where creatures are found to have the same issues as nobilities. Exemplifying, perhaps, there's no place like home. Meet fairies as they frolic and play the noble hearts and sway, posed in the recesses of night, and mystic lands of a faraway kingdom.

22 Characters

The Merchant of Venice

An angry Shylock brings to trial a merchant, over a lover's quarrel disrupted, demanding pounds of flesh. With no desires for even three times the amount, the Shylock demands his vengeance at heart.

22 Characters

The Merry Wives of Windsor
Mistresses and lords try and relate towards one another, as various important community figures come to have their word/seek the hostesses. Pleasantries are exchanged as a range of charms are expressed, until conversation resembled so to folly.

23 Characters

Much Ado About Nothing
Soldiery level consideration occupy the gossip, as several hostilities are summoned up, onto heart related matter. Also in conflict. The latter portion of the story lightens up to a women's home and pleasantries. Thereafter, a general search and care in actions, creating response phrasing poetic to the responses of leadership parading, until an end full of sensitivity asking gently questions, onto kisses

23 Characters

As You Like It
Troubled lower nobles venture about daily business, with some mild graces towards the ladies found. In need of relief or play, the Duke and family members take to the woods, where jests of drinking turn into troubled amusements, or warmth of a women's heart.

26 Characters

Troilus and Cressida

The infamous Greek battle for Troy. A large army arrives to take back the lost love of a humiliated foe. Both sides mobilize heroes onto the field, as soldiers and generals move to the side, and let strategies and fate take their course.

21+ Characters

All's Well That Ends Well

A tale of delightful, womanly gossip of a prestigious sort, until the French King has his word on the excellence of others. The story initially revolves around a strong willed countess, whose courteous pose and insight, reflect a nobility reflective of the house and court (council). Dialogue therein revolving around the councils rather, to exemplify (court counselling women).

25 Characters

Measure for Measure

Statesmen discourse leading with time to a personal reflection. Strolling Dukes and strong willed women occupy the background, where high-function status and family discourse intertwine within formalities (of administrative foresight, expression) observed.

24 Characters

Richard III

An in palace drama with King Richard the 3rd, Queen Elizabeth, and Queen Margret. Onto a haunting reunion, as the state processes royal executions.

61+ Characters

The Life and Death of King John
King John and Queen Elinor entertain the royal court, where a bastard has come to make his day. Strategic deployments of influence are exemplified, as the bastard plots about until alerts, alarm corruption has delivered trouble makers known.

24 Characters

Romeo and Juliet
Lovers emerge within a city gripped with two feuding houses apposed. As turmoil are caught in bitter heat, the lover's. Bliss and undying pledge becomes them, onto the eternal soul (of love and romance).

33 Characters

Othello
A hopeful Othello calls upon the favor of allies based on proposed merits, which called upon allies and foes to him. In a mixed response, allies and foes campaign both against Othello, becoming a bitter, personal tangle over a mislead love adventure representing the future of either fates

25 Characters

Macbeth
A desperate Macbeth ventures towards witches to tell fortune, returning to a castle haunted by ghost/old-spirits. Macbeth's worries become frightful nightmares, along the despair of the household around him.

39 Characters

Mark Antony and Cleopatra
The relations or affections of Mark Anthony and Cleopatra, onto the strategic interactions between Mark Anthony and Octavius. The discourse moves to the Octavius house, revealing Octavia, and later then, Pompey in the background. Overall the focus retains upon Mark Anthony, Cleopatra, and Octavius.

56+ Characters

Coriolanus
Citizens riot during a famine, while the state administrative intervenes and otherwise discourses the seriousness of the matter and war. Lady's calm the general ambience, until the sword is mobilized to defend the gates, , while the plight of people is nevertheless heard convincing Roman elites the problem is being found/fought within.

60 Characters

Pericles Prince of Tyre
A thoughtful/reflective Pericles interposes his good will and well-meaning nature, which leads him to visit fishermen friends, and onto state function. Pericles is then confronted, required to (take a plunge) to marry, embedding him deeper into ocean stock of sea life among sailors experience and merchant owners, investing his interest as babe, securing his destiny as then, future king

44 Characters

Cymbeline
Cymbeline, friend or loyalist to the first Caesars, is summoned into battle. Meanwhile there are personal matters to attend to within the noble house.

41 Characters

The Winter's Tale
A gossipy tale of high office, administrative daily insight onto the tender meaning of things and people an how they unite unwittingly at the discourse of their respected hierarchies of partnership. Profoundness therein inspiring the recounts of clown and child, as examples perhaps of what state administration and or nobility's company keeps.

34+ Characters

The Tempest
After an earth shattering storm, a fairy dwelling world is found. There magic and graces are there in song, glory and praises.

21 Characters

The Two Gentlemen of Verona
Loving beginnings, yet far too. General virtues going upwards in hierarchies, with overall chivalrous wits.

Twelfth Night
An evening in the company of sound gatherings, seemingly a docile manner recount version of noble delights. In similarities of the pose, composing an environment of insight and oversight.

Henry the 8th
Across chamber and palace, Dukes and lords, until Queen Katharine's and King Henry VIII's present their graces, conversing the Cardinal then. The signs then, an Elizabeth is born.

Richard II
King Richard the 2nd readies the armed forces at the sound of alarm, while later Henry IV is near for discussion. King Richard the 2nd and his groom.

Henry V
King Henry the 5th, as found across his palace, until a readiness for war. King Henry the 5th and the French King, with armies both have at it.

Henry VI, Part 1
Funeral of King Henry the 5th, Henry VI makes his approach to France. Henry VI fashions as thy lord protector.

Henry VI, Part 2
King Henry the 6th, where the Cardinal is seen mocking protectors with praise, as all the rage. Queen Margaret at King Henry VI, until the end.

Henry VI, Part 3
King Henry VI is busy fighting a succession of battles, France and England as having at it, yet again.

King Henry the 5th
King Henry 5 fight his way toward France, they reach the peaceful and loving responses of a French King.

Henry IV, Part 1
King Henry the 4th, from Palace to Pub, onto the battle fields again. Until there is no rebellion.

Henry IV, Part 2
Henry IV, from Palace, Priest and then tavern, he nevertheless finds some peace, after reflection. King Henry IV, and then King Henry V as fashionable by the end.

Titus Andronicus
A story of Romans and Goths, where roman sways give way. And then to see about Goths and proving worthiness.

28 Characters

Julius Caesar
Near the Final days of the 1st Caesar, and the continuation everlasting as through Octavius.

Hamlet
Hamlet, and his father the King, the father yet a Ghost. Hamlet, not so eager to join.

King Lear
King Lear, from palace to castle, to fighting the French in the field. After battle King Lear is in bed, the Doctor discourses, what lays then now, will have an impact upon the end.

Timon of Athens
A story set in Greece, a place of poets and cultured, good graces. From Arts and daily expressive, to political and charmed.

www.ingramcontent.com/pod-product-compliance
Lightning Source LLC
Chambersburg PA
CBHW071425080526
44587CB00014B/1743